A Bride
GOES WEST

By

NANNIE T. ALDERSON

and

HELENA HUNTINGTON SMITH

B Ald

74914

Drawings by J. O'H. Cosgrave II

UNIVERSITY OF NEBRASKA PRESS
LINCOLN AND LONDON

First Bison Book printing January, 1969
Most recent printing shown by first digit below:
15   16   17   18   19   20

Bison Book edition reprinted by arrangement with Helena Huntington Smith and Mrs. William Eaton.

FOREWORD

NANNIE TIFFANY ALDERSON is one of the last generation of American women who were pioneers. When they are all gone, there will be nobody left who will remember what it felt like to set up housekeeping two days' journey from a grocery store; or what were the problems of keeping a dirt floor clean. Mrs. Alderson, or "Domo" as she is universally called, is old enough to remember it all, and young enough— she was eighty-one her last birthday—to remember it in a very lively fashion. She acquired her nickname, or rather her title, some thirty-odd years ago, through the efforts of her first grandchild to pronounce "grandma."

Because her daughter Patty is married to Bill Eaton, Domo lives today on Eaton's ranch, oldest and best known of dude ranches, outside of Sheridan, Wyoming. Still thoroughly independent, she has her own house, where she serves fruitades and "swizzles" to dudes who ride the three miles down from the ranch on a summer's morning. Tiny and frail as she is to look at, she has the energy of a woman half her age and twice her size, and will still lift mammoth kettles of boiling wild-plum jam, or will tote pails of

water around, unless someone stops her. Of course,
her home is built of logs. She has never lived in a
frame house since she was married, except for the
few years she spent in Miles City. And she has gotten
up at five o'clock every morning of her life, until the
last few years. Since she is always exceedingly dainty
and smartly dressed, with nothing rugged about her
to outward view, you would never guess that she was
a pioneer woman except for something about her
eyes. They look at you very straight, without flinch-
ing. Few women reared in luxury have eyes like that;
all the surviving women I have met, who have lived
against Domo's hard background, have them.

Many of those who tackled the hardships of a new
country in the early days were poor folk, farmers,
people who had known nothing but hard living even
before they went west. But others, among them Nannie Alderson, were bred up to silver and old mahog-
any, pretty clothes, servants and leisure. How could
such girls have turned their backs so gladly on all
that women live for, or think they live for, to find ful-
fillment between log walls, in a life barren of everything but living? That is the riddle of American
pioneering. When you know the answer, you will
know one reason why we are a great people. And
Nannie Alderson's story throws a good deal of light
on the question.

She is a natural story-teller. For years she has been

telling her tales of the cowboys and the children, the Indians, the Eastern visitors and the animals who peopled the domestic scene on a small Montana ranch; and these tales of hers have made the wild West seem a good deal less wild and more human. I have put the stories together for her in this book, but they are still told in her own words.

HELENA HUNTINGTON SMITH.

A BRIDE GOES WEST

Chapter I

LIKE MANY OF THOSE WHO SETTLED THE FAR WEST, my husband and I were both Southerners.

I was born in the village of Union, West Virginia, on September 14, 1860. My father, Captain Hugh Tiffany of Monroe County, West Virginia, or Virginia as it was then, was killed at the beginning of the First Battle of Manassas, and was said to be the first southern officer who fell in the war. He was a young lawyer not quite twenty-seven years old when the war came, and he at once formed a volunteer company of his old schoolmates and friends, the cream of Monroe County. The village gave a banquet for them the night before they left, and a small silk Confederate flag, which the ladies of the village had made, was presented to them on the occasion. My father made a speech of acceptance—and a very flowery one I'm sure—saying that wherever the company marched the flag would go, in honor of the fair hands that had made it, and so forth. Long afterwards it went with me to Montana, where it was one of the few things saved when my house was burned by Indians.

Mother married again before I was four, and one of the first things I remember is her wedding day. I remember my colored nurse taking me down into the kitchen where old Uncle Caesar was getting the wedding breakfast ready; I have also kept an impression of being underfoot, and not wanted. Then I was taken up to a room where my mother was sitting in her riding habit, talking to a gentleman dressed in black broadcloth, who must have been the bridegroom. She was married in riding clothes, because she was to ride to her new home. It seemed to me that one of the most beautiful things I had ever seen was the black velvet turban with two pearl pins in it, which rested on her light, golden-brown hair.

But it appeared that I wasn't wanted in that room

either, for the next thing I remember was sitting on the stairs watching the guests arrive. It was June, 1864, and my uncle was home on furlough from the war. He picked me up and carried me into the parlor, setting me down on a side table at the back of the room. I don't remember being much impressed by the ceremony, but I do remember playing with the snuffers of a pair of silver candelabra, while all the people were quiet. Years later those snuffers and the candelabra too went with me to Montana.

They had told me that mother was going to send for me after her wedding trip. I waited, it seemed, a long time, but the summons came at last, and I went in front of an old mulatto woman on a white horse, to visit my mother's new plantation home. The family always spoke of it as Nannie's long journey—it was five miles. After staying a few days, I was taken back to Union to live with my grandmother in the village, and for many years thereafter my mother had me only for visits in the summertime.

She couldn't have been over twenty-one at the time of this marriage. My stepfather, Colonel Rowan, was a good many years older than she, and was in politics. I know he served in the Confederate legislature all during the war. Through him, I acquired a family consisting of a stepbrother and two stepsisters older than I, with whom I played on those summer visits to the plantation. My stepbrother, Andrew Rowan, was to gain fame in the Spanish-American War by carrying the message to Garcia; he stands out in my childish memory as a lordly and awful being, who somehow hypnotized us younger ones into doing his will. We would roam the woods gathering berries or chestnuts—my stepsister Betty and I, and several pickaninnies—and when we came home with our pailful, Andrew would offer to divide them for us.

His way of dividing was to say: "Here's one for Nannie and one for me; one for Betty and one for me"—and so on till he took half of all we had gathered. I don't know why we let him do it!

In the winter my stepsister Betty, eighteen months older, came in and stayed in town with me and we went to school together. As I looked at it, this arrangement had a serious drawback; it obliged me to go to school the year round. The public school near the plantation kept in summer, when the roads were better and the children could get there more easily, and my stepfather, perhaps for political reasons, made his own children go. Later on in Union I went to a seminary where the girls were taught a smattering of music and French and other polite subjects, but not much of any of them, so that when I had to support myself years later, the only thing I knew was to take boarders. I didn't even graduate from the seminary, because when I was fifteen my stepfather decided that Betty and I had reached the stage where we had boys in our heads, and it was a waste of money to pay for any more schooling for us.

In spite of my grandmother's devotion I was a lonely child, for she was deaf, and talking to her was difficult. My mother was a very pretty woman, fond of dress and society, and I was always a disappointment to her because I was neither. Not that I was bad-looking—but my stepsister Betty was the pretty one, and mother liked to hear people say, as they often did, that Betty looked more like her than her own child.

Mother, though a southern lady of the floweriest tradition, was also a realist. She had a fondness for pinchback jewelry—which was our name for artificial diamonds set in paste—and she calmly ignored the rule of the day which said that no lady ever wore it. When she went to the city she would go to one of the cheap stores where it was sold, and pick out some handsome-looking pieces. Later she would wear these along with her real jewels, saying in her soft, pretty voice: "No one would evah dare say Mrs. Rowan wore pinchback jewelry."

She also used rouge—though southern society considered rouged cheeks the hallmark of a fast woman, if the wearer were found out. I made the discovery by accident one day when I was a little girl. I was rummaging about in the room which my mother used when she came to town—for I was a great rummager, as I think lonely children often are—and in the drawer of the dressing table I came upon a little box of crimson paste. I suppose I sensed what it was for— but I had no idea of the scandal it would cause when I took it to school and showed it to my schoolmates!

The year I was sixteen a new world opened up before me. My father's sister, Elizabeth Tiffany, had married a Mr. Symms and had pioneered in Kansas in the Fifties. On one of her periodic visits to Virginia she stopped to see me, because I wanted to know my father's people. The result was an invitation to visit her in Atchison, Kansas, from September to June.

What an experience that was! Kansas then was the West. I felt that the very air there was easier to breathe. In Union you had to have your pedigree with you to be accepted anywhere, but in Atchison it didn't matter a bit who your ancestors were or what you did for a living; if you were nice you were nice. What impressed me most was the fact that a girl could work in an office or a store, yet that wouldn't keep her from being invited to the nicest homes or marrying one of the nicest boys. This freedom to work seemed to me a wonderful thing. I wanted to do something useful myself, as I felt keenly my dependence on my stepfather. But Auntie wouldn't let me; she knew my mother would never consent.

So many little foolish conventions that we were

brought up on at home didn't apply in Atchison. There was much less formality there; when people went visiting they took their darning or their knitting with them in the friendly old-fashioned way—but when I tried it after returning to West Virginia, mother was shocked. In Union on Sunday we were never allowed to open the piano nor to visit anybody except relatives; in Kansas we all did as we pleased about these matters, and when I remonstrated with my cousin for playing a piece of popular music, she was able to retort: "I don't think it's any more wrong than it is for you to sit on the porch and talk to boys on a Sunday afternoon!"

I had to admit that she was right. But the boys all worked, and Sunday was the only day they could come.

On this visit I first met my husband. One evening in June, 1877 I was invited to take supper and spend the night with a Baptist preacher's family named Alderson, who were West Virginians like ourselves. There were several brothers in the home, and three or four girls had been invited. After a jolly supper one of the boys excused himself from the parlor and went out on the porch to smoke a cigar.

In a minute he was back, saying excitedly: "Mother, Walt's home!"

This announcement produced a great effect. "Walt," I learned, was a brother who had run away

to Texas when he was twelve or thirteen years old,
and they hadn't seen him for nine years.

They made him come inside—a cowboy in sombrero and chaps. We girls were not impressed; we
thought he was funny-looking. I remember that he
was rather silent and ill at ease, and soon excused himself, saying he was going to bed. In the morning the
brother brought the startling news that "Walt" had
not slept in bed, but had gotten up in the night, taken
a quilt, and lain down on the floor of the bedroom.
This strange visitor, they said, had come up with a
herd of cattle to Dodge City, the wild, tough cowtown
which was then a northern terminus of the great cattle
trail from Texas. He had left the house very early,
before any of us were up, and I didn't see him again,
except once at a crystal wedding party, before going
back to Virginia.

Much later I found out what lay behind his sudden
appearance that night in his strange cowboy dress.
To begin with, his birthplace was only twenty miles
from mine, at Alderson, West Virginia. But he was
five years older than I and his father, an anti-slavery
preacher, had moved out in the rush to settle Kansas
before I was born. There he built one of the first
Baptist churches in the state. There were six sons and
a daughter in the family, and Walter was next to the
youngest.

His parents were conscientious, high-minded

people who thought their first duty was to the church, not to their children and home. There was a good deal of strictness about certain matters, such as the observance of Sunday, but Walter was always wild and irrepressible. The people in Atchison used to tell a story of his riding home on a horse afternoons, behind his father; Mr. Alderson, Senior, kept a bookstore in town during the week, and Walter was ordered to come to the store after school, so as not to get into mischief playing with bad boys. For years afterwards Atchison used to smile over the picture they made; the dignified white-bearded preacher with his stove-pipe hat, and the imp of a boy perched behind him, facing the horse's tail, making all kinds of faces and comical gestures as they journeyed along the street, while the preacher bowed gravely from side to side, acknowledging what he took to be smiles of greeting to himself.

Mrs. Alderson was too busy with her church work to give much attention to his bringing up, so much of the time he was left in the charge of his older brothers, who were allowed to punish him. He resented this, and at thirteen he ran away to Texas. Two other boys ran away with him; their fathers went after them and brought them home, but Mr. Alderson, Senior, was very wise. He said: "No, since that is what he wants, let him go and learn for himself."

Texas in the late Sixties was wild and rough, the

very place to appeal to rebellious spirits. I have often
wished that I remembered more of Mr. Alderson's experiences there. I know that when he first went down
there he got a job washing dishes for his keep. Later
his boots gave out, and his first piece of luck was finding five dollars, with which he bought new ones. At
one time he drove a stage coach during the night; I
can't recall where, only that the little town at one end
of his run was called Sweet Home. That has always
seemed to me a lovely name. He told me that every
morning at sunup, near the end of his long night's
drive, a mocking bird would be singing in a certain
liveoak tree when he went by. He came to look for it,
and if the bird wasn't there, the day would be spoiled
for him.

He had always been good with horses, so he drifted
naturally into becoming a cowboy, and went up the
trail to Kansas. He spoke of it as a hard school, with
poor food and much exposure to the weather. I believe he had been up to Dodge City before, but on this
trip, when he got up there with the herd, it came to
him all of a sudden that he would go home and see his
people.

I spent a year at home in West Virginia after our
first meeting; then, when I was seventeen, I went back
to Atchison to stay with my aunt again, remaining
this time for four years.

I did not see Mr. Alderson at once on my second

visit. Although he had stayed in Atchison, he didn't live at home, but had rooms downtown, where he went around with a fast horse-racing crowd. It may sound strange today to speak of horse-racing in Kansas, but the western part of the state at that time was not far from its wide-open frontier days, and the sporting element still held its own.

I should probably never have seen him again if his father had not taken ill. There were no nurses then; neighbors helped each other, and Auntie and I took turns at looking after the old gentleman. On a night when I was sitting up, Walter came home. He owned a half interest in a race mare which he took on the circuit, and he had been in Kansas City racing this horse when his father grew worse, and they telegraphed him to come.

He was tall—just half an inch under six feet—blue-eyed, and of a fine appearance. Later, when he came to Virginia for our wedding, my mother, who loved beauty in man, woman or child, said to me: "Why didn't you tell me he's good-looking?" I replied that I'd preferred to let her find that out for herself.

For many nights after his arrival in Atchison we sat up together by the old gentleman's bedside, or talked quietly in the next room. In those talks he told me much about his early life, and one thing he said I have always remembered; that he had never known any pleasure in his home until I was in it. I believe that was one thing that gave him such a strong feeling for home afterwards. He told me, too, that he had made up his mind never to marry, but that I had changed it. He was already planning to go out and start a cattle ranch in Montana, and he asked me if I would be afraid to share that kind of life with him. I told him I wasn't afraid, and we became engaged soon after his father died.

My aunt and the relatives in Atchison did not approve the match at first. This was not because he was taking me to the unsettled West; they all thought the ranching business had a wealthy future, so that was looked upon as a good thing. No, they disapproved because of his wild reputation. But I had perfect confidence in him, believing then, as I do now, that it's not what a man has done before marriage that counts, it is what he does after.

I wanted to see my grandmother again before going so far away, so I went home to West Virginia and spent the next year there, getting ready to be married. How often I blessed Auntie in Atchison who had taught me to sew, and had also instilled what little smattering of common sense I had. I made all my trousseau myself. Thanks to Auntie I did have sense enough to make my underthings plain according to the standards of the day—so they had some pretense at suitability to the life I was planning to lead. When I had first arrived in Atchison my petticoats were like mother's—a mass of lace, and frills upon frills. Auntie explained that this made too much ironing for one servant, and she taught me to make simpler ones. So now I made my trousseau petticoats with just a single deep ruffle tucked solid to hold the starch, and a band of lace whipped to the ruffle. Mother thought them dreadfully plain, but when I had to iron them I thought them elaborate enough.

I made my own wedding dress of white embroidered mull, and I earned the money to buy my wedding veil. This was how it happened. My grandfather had had a body servant, Alec, who was freed at the end of the war with the other slaves. He went North and prospered, becoming steward of a hotel in the White Mountains. In all those years, however, he never lost his loyal devotion to our family, and in 1882 he visited Union, bringing with him his wife, a smart young colored woman of whom he was very proud. She needed a new dress while in Union, and he was humiliated because none of the dressmakers, who of course were white, would make one for her. He told me about it one day, almost with tears in his eyes.

I said: "Why, Alec, I'll make your wife's dress, gladly. And what's more, I'll let you pay me for it."

He said: "Miss Nannie, would you do that?" I never have seen a man so touchingly grateful. So I made the dress, and earned my wedding veil.

While I was at home making these preparations,

Mr. Alderson was in Montana hunting a site for a ranch. His partner was Mr. John Zook of St. Joe, Missouri, a young man who shared his interest in horses and the out-of-doors. The two of them had owned this race mare together, and when they decided to go into ranching, the arrangement was that Mr. Zook was to provide the capital while my husband furnished the experience. The Northern Pacific was built as far as Miles City, Montana, and Mr. Alderson arrived on one of the first trains to come through from the East.

He stopped at a road ranch up Tongue River which was run by some people named Lays. That year the buffalo were still so thick that Mrs. Lays had only to say: "Mr. Alderson, we're out of meat"; and he would go out and find a herd and kill a calf, all just as easily as a man would butcher a yearling steer in his own pasture. Yet when I came out, one year later, there was nothing left of those great bison herds, which had covered the continent, but carcasses. I saw them on my first drive out to the ranch, and they were lying thick all over the flat above our house, in all stages of decay. So wasteful were the hunters, they had not even removed the tongues, though the latter were choice meat.

The summer after I came out Mr. Alderson killed the last buffalo ever seen in our part of Montana. A man staying with us was out fishing when he saw this lonesome old bull wandering over the hills and gullies above our house—the first live buffalo seen in many months. He came home and reported it, saying: "Walt, why don't you go get him?" And next morning Mr. Alderson did go get him.

That afternoon he suggested that we take the spring wagon and go up to where the old bull had fallen. There he lay in the green brush at the bottom of a draw—the last of many millions—with the bushes propping him up so that he looked quite lifelike. I had brought my scissors, and I snipped a sackfull of the coarse, curly hair from his mane to stuff a pillow with.

I am afraid that the conservation of buffalo, or of any other wild game, simply never occurred to the westerner of those days.

The site Mr. Alderson chose for a ranch was near the mouth of Lame Deer Creek where it runs into the Rosebud, some sixty miles above the place where the Rosebud joins the Yellowstone. Crook had fought the Indians on the Rosebud only six years before, and Custer had marched up it, to cross over the divide and be slaughtered with all his command at the battle of the Little Big Horn. I had read about all this when it happened, and had seen a picture of Custer with his long yellow hair in one of our Southern papers, when I was just a young girl. I had been terribly and painfully impressed, never dreaming that I should some day live so near the battlefield, even visit it, and walk on ground that had been stained by his blood.

With the ranch selected and the cattle bought, Mr. Zook sold the race horse in Kansas and went out to the ranch to take over, while Mr. Alderson spent his share of the proceeds on coming East. We were married at my mother's house in Union, on April 4, 1883.

For weeks and weeks it had rained, as it can rain only in the West Virginia mountains, but that morning the sun came out, and I was awakened by my niece's voice exclaiming: "Why, the sun is shining on Aunt Nannie's wedding day!"

The servants' faces were all wreathed in smiles.

The ceremony was at ten, and in the afternoon Mr. Alderson and I went across the mountains by stage to Alderson, where we were to be entertained by his relatives before we took the train. As we went down into the valley toward Alderson we saw the sun setting in a great mass of gold and purple clouds; before we were through dinner it was raining again, and we heard it on the train that night. Mother wrote me afterwards that it rained for weeks.

On our way west we paid farewell visits to civilization at Chicago and St. Paul. Farther on the train stopped for an hour at Mandan, South Dakota, to enable the passengers to see a wonderful collection of mounted animals. The great heads and horns of the beasts of the prairie made a deep impression on me, since I was so soon to be living among them.

I went with romantic ideas of being a helpmeet to a man in a new country, but I was sadly ill-equipped when it came to carrying them out. Before I left Union a dear old lady had taught me how to make hot rolls, but except for that one accomplishment I knew no more of cooking than I did of Greek. Hot rolls, plus a vague understanding that petticoats ought to be plain, were my whole equipment for conquering the West.

Chapter II

I HAD BEEN PREPARED FOR MILES CITY AHEAD OF time, so I was not surprised by the horses hitched to rails along the store fronts, the wooden sidewalks and unpaved streets, nor was I surprised that every other building was a saloon. Mr. Alderson had told me it was a pretty hoorah place. He didn't want me to go out alone, even in the daytime—not that I wouldn't be perfectly safe, but I might run into a drunken crowd or a fight.

We stopped at the Macqueen House, which was headquarters for cattlemen and for men who were planning to become cattlemen. It was homey enough in one way, but it was a poorly built, wooden structure; and as the only bath was off the barber shop, I had to bathe in the wash basin just as I did later at the ranch. The walls were so thin that you could hear every sound from one end to the other, with the result that I overheard several masculine conversations which both fascinated and embarrassed me. Once I heard a man say: "You know, there isn't a decent waitress in this house"—which shocked me because the waitresses had been very kind. I could hardly believe it.

Miles City was teeming with men who were going into the cattle business; many were friends of my husband, and they came from all parts of the United States. Among those whom Mr. Alderson brought upstairs to introduce to me I remember men from Chicago, from Pennsylvania, from Maryland, and several from Texas. One was a lawyer from Boston, Mr. Loud—or Judge Loud as he later became; he was planning to raise cattle until he had saved enough money to keep him during the lean years while he was building a practice. They were all gallant enough to be greatly interested in a wife who was planning to live on a ranch with her husband.

I must have bragged of my one accomplishment—

hot rolls—for they all declared they were tired of baking powder biscuit and sour dough bread, and they all announced: "We're coming to see you." So part of our preparation for the ranch was going to a bake shop the night before we left and buying a bottle of starter for my yeast. We went to bed leaving the bottle corked, and in the middle of the night it exploded with a loud "Pop."

Mr. Alderson's first thought was that someone had fired off a gun; and he jumped up and took his six-shooter and started out to investigate. The next moment we heard the sizzle-sizzle-sizzle of the yeast running out of the bottle. In a moment it was all over the room, and even on the dress I'd been planning to wear.

But when we told about the catastrophe in the morning, one of the stockmen said: "I'm still coming for those hot rolls and you're not going out there without that yeast." So he went out and got a tin bucket full, which we took with us.

Mr. Alderson had assured my mother and grand-mother that I could go on to Bozeman where he had bought the cattle, and stay with friends there while our new house was being finished. I had different ideas, however, and on the train I had told him that I wanted to go on with him. He was very ready to be convinced.

So we left Miles City April seventeenth, with a hundred-mile journey ahead of us which would take two days. We were driving behind two horses in a spring wagon, which was like a buckboard but very much more comfortable. Already the grass had started, and the country was prettily tinged with green. But it was a big and bare country, with only scattering pine trees and the cottonwoods in the river bottoms to break its vast monotony. In all the years of my marriage, I never had trees over my head; they could have been planted, but we never lived long enough in one place for them to grow.

We made our first noon halt at Piper Dan's, a road ranch thirty-five miles out of Miles City, where the Tongue River mail stage changed horses. Dan was a bearded old Scotchman who played the bagpipes— hence his name. If he had any other no one knew it. His place was clean enough, but rough and untidy, and the walls of his two-room log house were papered from end to end with the pink pages of Police Gazettes. I'd been warned I'd better not look at them, so of course, as soon as the men went out to put up the horses, look at them was the first thing I did. They were not as bad as I expected. Today those buxom women in their black or flesh-colored tights would seem almost modestly clad.

For dinner we had a buffalo steak, cut from one of the last buffalo in that part of Montana. The rest of the week was the usual bachelor fare of boiled pota-

toes, dried fruit and sourdough bread. Dan was supposed to be a woman-hater, but he was most kind,
even to cooking the one egg for "the missus" which
his hen had laid that day; and I dried the dishes for
him while the team was being hitched. I was the first
bride who had ever stopped there.

That night we stayed at a second road ranch on
Tongue River. We had a comfortable room to ourselves with a good bed, which the hostess must have
given up to us, since the ordinary accommodations
consisted of a kind of bunk room which was occupied
that night by fully fifteen men. They were all young,
nearly all seemed to be Easterners, and they were all
going into the cattle business. Next morning at breakfast we all sat at one long table, and they talked of
nothing but cattle, horses and prices. Everyone, it
seemed, was making fabulous sums of money or was
about to make them; no one thought of losses; and
for the next year my husband and I were to breathe
that air of optimism and share all those rose-colored
expectations.

The second day of our trip was beautiful when we
started out, though before we arrived it had clouded
over and begun to snow. After coming sixty-five or
seventy miles up Tongue River, we crossed over the
divide to the Rosebud, then went on down a long
gulch to Lame Deer. One of my first lessons as a
western wife was that location in that almost unin-

habited country was not a matter of cities and roads, but of rivers and divides. Rivers, like women, were few, and they gained in importance proportionally, while the location of every tiny creek might be a matter of life-and-death importance to men and animals alike.

We picnicked at noon, eating lunch beside Tongue River while the horses were fed oats and grazed on the new green grass. The scene was wild and picturesque enough, but I was feeling the effects of the journey, and besides was greatly troubled by a question which had begun to form in my mind. All that day and the day before we had kept passing low, cheerless-looking log shacks, mud-daubed, with weeds sticking up out of dirt roofs. They looked primitive and uninviting enough to be the habitations of Indians, or of animals, and my heart sank lower and lower as I saw them.

Finally I screwed up the courage to ask: "Is ours as bad as that?"

"Worse," Mr. Alderson answered. "Ours is as unattractive as a shack can be."

Then he explained again what I already knew; that our house hadn't even been built for us but was just a maverick shack, as he called it, that had been thrown together as a shelter for some men who were getting out railroad ties. The tie cutters had been working in the Wolf Mountains, some miles above our home, and the idea was to float the ties down the Rosebud to the Yellowstone, where they would be used to build the Northern Pacific. A second group of men was camped near the mouth of Lame Deer to watch and see that they didn't jam. But there wasn't enough water in the Rosebud, and the scheme fell through. So an abandoned loggers' camp became my first Montana home.

In the late afternoon we came out of the mouth of a gulch down which we had been traveling. A huddle of log buildings lay below us on the flat, and as I watched, a man on horseback burst out of it, galloping across the valley. I was told that it was one of our cowboys, and that he was probably going after the milk cow. Two men climbed down from a partly completed log house—our house-to-be. Then a fourth man whom I recognized as Johnny appeared in the door of a low cabin. So this was home.

In a minute I was unfolding my cramped limbs and being helped out of the spring wagon, and then I was being introduced to "Old Uncle—the best logger in Montana," and to "Baltimore Bill—the best man ever seen on the end of a whipsaw." They were building our new house. Then the cowboy, Brown Taliaferro, came riding back and greeted me as "Miss Tiffany," which made everybody laugh and eased the stiffness.

The first sight of my temporary home was not reassuring—a dirt-roofed cabin, hardly any taller than a man, with one door and only *one window*! In this country where windows had to be hauled many miles they were usually used sparingly, one being made to do the work of two—a half to each room. An immense pair of elk antlers hung over the door, one prong supporting a human skull which was perforated with bullet holes. The skull, I later learned, had been picked up on the battle ground of Lame Deer; whether it was Indian or white no one knew, but most of the bullet holes had been put there in the course of target practice by the boys.

Indoors waited a pleasant shock. On our arrival in Miles City Johnny Zook had met us, expecting to take my husband back to the ranch with him while I went on to Bozeman. As soon as he learned of my intention of coming to the ranch, he went on out ahead of us to fix things up for my coming. He had said merely: "I'm going out to take down the variety actresses off the walls." But when I saw what a home he had made of that little shack, I had to admit that few women could have done as well.

A bright fire was burning in the stone fireplace, and the dirt floor was covered with a clean new wagon sheet of white canvas. Over that were laid several beautifully tanned skins—a buffalo robe, a mountain lion, a gray wolf, a coyote and two red fox pelts more worthy to be used for a lady's neckpiece than for rugs. (Later I hung those fox skins on the wall.) Johnny had even found a white bedspread—as I later had cause to regret, for our bedroom was also the family living room, the bed did double duty as a couch, and I never could keep that bedspread clean. A gray army blanket, hung across an opening in the logs, made a door between the bedroom and the kitchen. I was told to lie down and rest while the men got supper ready. I gratefully did so, but was too excited and tired to sleep.

Just before supper my husband came in, to explain that Uncle and Baltimore Bill (so called because he talked so much about Baltimore, where he had once been), had been worrying because neither possessed a coat other than the kind worn in winter for warmth. Going coatless was a custom of the country; would I excuse the boys if they came to the table in their shirt-sleeves?

I said Yes, of course I would. But when I did go out and sit down to table in the dirt-floored kitchen, with those grizzled coatless men in their grimy-looking flannel work shirts they had worn all day, a wave of homesickness came over me.

It soon disappeared in enjoyment of one of the best suppers I ever ate—hot biscuits, venison and bacon, potato chips, evaporated fruit and coffee. That men could cook was something new under the sun to me, but the men in Montana could and did, and most

of what I learned during my first years as a housewife
I learned from them.

This first meal was a product of bachelor team
work in the kitchen, and as such was typical. My husband was the biscuit maker and meat cook; Brown
made the gravy and the coffee, while our partner's
specialty was saratoga chips, on which he spent all
the care and artistry of a French chef, putting one or
two in the fat at a time, and bringing them on the
table piping hot.

The table was the let-down lid of a chuck box, such
as was used on roundup wagons. This crude kitchen
cabinet, the stove, and some home-made three-legged
stools were the sole furnishings of the kitchen that
night, but next day Uncle was turned over to me, to
build a table and benches. I had brought enough
white oilcloth to cover the top, and when it was set
for our supper the second night with bright red
doilies, my grandmother's silver, an old-fashioned
"lazy Susan" in the center with vinegar, salt, pepper
and mustard bottles; and two delicate china cups and
saucers to raise the tone, I felt I had made a real
stride toward home-making in the West.

After supper my husband said: "When the dishes
are done we'll open our trunks and treat you to some
cake and maple sugar from West Virginia, and Mrs.
Alderson will play and sing for you."

I had brought my guitar. But when we lifted the

lid of the trunk, a tragic sight met our eyes. The body was broken straight across the neck, and gapped like an old rhinoceros' mouth. There, I thought, went all hope of music in the long months to come. But my first lesson in making the best of things came then and there, for my husband and Johnny took strips of surgeon's tape, which they kept handy in case of accident, and they taped it together so that in tone, if not in looks, it was almost as good as new.

I had little voice, but my listeners were hungry for music and no prima-donna ever enjoyed so heartwarming a triumph as I did that night. I won old Uncle's heart with three Scotch ballads, which I murdered over and over again for him. By the end of the evening they all had their favorites. Mr. Zook liked a very sentimental poem of Byron's set to music, and Brown's choice was a teary song about a little child who was left alone by his parents. The house caught fire and flames crackled around him; each verse ended with the sad refrain, "Lost in the fire"—but in the final stanza rescue came, and the last line of all was "Saved from the fire." Particularly touching was the part where his baby voice lisped: "God told me you would come." I sang a good deal for cowboys afterwards, and that song was always their favorite.

Next morning I was told that old Uncle was making me a chair, which wouldn't turn over as the three-legged stools did. He came in presently with it. Certainly it was in no danger of upsetting. The four legs set under the seat sprawled at safe angles, an ox bow made the back, and the whole thing was covered with coyote skins. It was not only hideous; it was also the most uncomfortable chair I have ever sat in. But I wouldn't have hurt old Uncle's feelings for anything.

One question had troubled me all the way out to Montana: Would the ranch be equipped with a certain humble but necessary structure in the back yard? I had heard somewhere that men living alone and very primitively weren't apt to bother with such a nicety. And I was terribly afraid that now, with a woman coming, they might not think to build one. I worried over this during all those days on the train, but I had been brought up with such modesty that I couldn't bring myself to mention it to my husband. Finally, after we were in Miles City, I did screw up the courage to ask him about it one night. I don't know whether I was more shocked or relieved when Mr. Alderson laughed out loud.

"I knew all the time you were worrying about that," said the unfeeling man. "I just wouldn't help you out!"

I'm sure mine was the most wonderful structure of the kind ever built. It was made of boards which Uncle and Baltimore Bill had whipsawed out by hand; a most delicate and difficult operation, and one resorted to only in the absence of sawmills. All the lumber for our new house had to be whipsawed. The log is laid over the top of a pit, and two men at either end of a long saw cut out the planks one at a time. Uncle thought so much of his precious lumber that he couldn't bear to have a foot of it wasted, and so refused to trim off the ends of the boards used in the out-house—though, as Mr. Alderson told him, he wasn't saving anything that way, because the long ends would be sure to warp. This they did, and curled in all directions. No roof could be put over such a crazy thing, and all that summer and fall it stood open to the sky.

Chapter III

THE IGNORANCE OF BRIDES HAS BEEN A SUBJECT OF jokes probably ever since the days of Mother Eve. My own ignorance as I look back upon it seems incredible—and like Eve I had to learn housekeeping in a wilderness. If I had married at home in West Virginia I should at least have had kindly neighbor women to turn to for advice, and I should have had stores where I could buy things to cover a few of my mistakes. As it was I was a hundred horse-and-buggy miles from a loaf of baker's bread or a paper of pins. And with one unpleasant pair of exceptions, I didn't see a white woman from April to July.

The exceptions, our only women neighbors, lived four miles away up Lame Deer Creek. My husband had told me about this family from Idaho who had moved in above us about a year before, and were running a few cattle. When they came there were a mother, father, and two sons, one of whom was married to a widow with three children, but the father had died the previous winter, and as my husband had the only lumber nearer than a hundred miles, he had furnished boards, made the coffin and helped bury the old man. He thought the women would feel kindly toward us and would, in any case, be glad to make a little extra money by doing our washing. So the first ride I took after reaching the ranch was to go and see this family and make arrangements.

When we rode up to their cabin the entire family trooped out to greet us. If I had expected a neighborly welcome, I found out I was mistaken. The mother was about six feet tall, dressed in a mother hubbard wrapper of calico with her late husband's straw hat on her head. She had iron grey hair cut squarely off on a line with the biggest ears I ever saw on any human, and her beady black eyes leveled on me with that "Well, what is your business?" expression that stops just short of hostility. The man looked like his mother but had a more kindly appearance. The daughter-in-law was a meek pale woman with two children clinging to her skirts, and throughout the interview she had nothing to say. It was plain that the older woman was the boss.

She eyed me from the top of my Eastern-made riding cap to the pointed toe of my boots, and I felt she was saying to herself: "This is a little fool, and she shall pay for it." When we told her we hoped she would do our washing, she said, boring holes in me with those beady eyes:

"You can furnish soap and starch, send the clothes up and Sadie will do the washing for ten cents apiece. We won't do the ironing at any price."

Feeling faint, I accepted. As Aunt Rose, our colored laundress down south, had done our entire family washing and ironing for years for five dollars a month, I felt that we were being robbed. I felt that way more than ever when the first bill was ten dollars and eighty cents. Clearly, our washerwoman would soon own our entire herd of cattle if I didn't learn to wash.

The next week when my husband was away on Tongue River buying horses I announced to the rest of the "family" that I was going to do the washing, and even invited the boys to put in their soiled things. I had never done a washing in my life and supposed, in my ignorance, that all it required was willing hands and soap. I knew nothing about hard water—but I soon learned.

For a guide to housekeeping in the West I had brought a cook book and housekeeping manual which our dear old pastor at home had given me for a wedding present. This book, written by a Southern gentlewoman for Southern gentlewomen, didn't contain a single cake recipe that called for fewer than six eggs. I now opened it to the section on laundry, and the first sentence that met my eye was as follows: "Before starting to wash it is essential to have a large, light, airy laundry with at least seven tubs."

I had one tub, a boiler and a dishpan. But for air and light at least I was well off, since my laundry was the shady north end of the shack and took in the whole of Montana. I threw the book under the bunk bed and put all my best clothes in the boiler. I didn't use half enough soap, and the water was very alkaline. My white under-things turned a dingy yellow and came out covered with gummy black balls of alkali as big as a small pea and bigger, which stuck to the iron. I shall never forget that washing as long as I live.

The boys did their best to help. One of them got dinner, and the others helped me to wring the clothes out of the hot water. I was grateful for their efforts and their sympathy, but as they didn't know any more about laundry than I did, it was a case of the blind leading the blind. I had so little sense, I didn't even know enough to pour cold water over the boiling clothes to cool them, and neither did the rest of them. We wrung them out hot, until my fingers were bleeding around the nails. There was no clothesline, so one of the boys stretched a lariat in the yard, but there were no clothespins either, and when a wind came up it blew down half of the wash into the sawdust which covered the premises. In the midst of all this Sadie, the neighbor's daughter-in-law, came to call, I think to find out why I hadn't sent the washing that week. Humiliation was forgotten in the relief of being able to sit down.

Back home in West Virginia I had thought myself quite a housewife. Mother was ill a great deal and I carried the keys, feeling very proud as I went about with her key basket, unlocking closets and giving things out. But out here I found that I didn't know, as they say, straight up. On the ranch we had meat without end, milk, and butter (if I made it), and later a few vegetables. Every single other necessity of life came from Miles City. Once a year when the men went in to ship their cattle they laid in supplies— hundred-pound sacks of flour and sugar, huge tins of Arbuckle coffee, sides of bacon, evaporated fruits and canned goods by the case. What you forgot you did without. I don't know how many times in those first months I thought: "Oh, if we'd only remembered" this or that.

We had plenty of canned corn and canned tomatoes, but the fruits were a luxury. Everyone in the country lived out of cans, and you would see a great heap of them outside of every little shack. But we always had a barrel for ours. I had to learn to cook and have a semblance of variety on the table with just what we had on hand. With no experience and no women to turn to, I don't know what I'd have done if it hadn't been for the friendly helpfulness of men.

I couldn't get over it. Back home, if we were without a cook, my stepfather would drive down into the colored section and hire a new one, but he wouldn't dream of going into the kitchen, even to carry a pail of water, and all the men were the same. But in Montana that first spring there would always be three or four in the kitchen getting a meal—Mr. Alderson, Mr. Zook, one of the cowboys and myself. I had Mr. Alderson's thoughtfulness to thank for this in the first instance, because they had been cooking before I came and he had warned them that they were not to cease doing their share. But they were very willing. I would often have to get a meal at odd hours, for one of our own boys or for a visitor who might arrive in the middle of the afternoon after riding fifty miles since breakfast. He'd be hungry and would have to be fed without waiting for supper, but I never got one of these extra meals without help. The men would always make the fire and grind the coffee and cut the meat, and would be so concerned about troubling me. The boys taught me what they could. For instance, I learned from them how to make a very good rice pudding without any eggs. They would take the uncooked rice with a lot of raisins and currants and sugar and would cook it in milk, so long and slowly that it turned caramel-brown. They would mix it in a milk pan and set it in the oven, and every so often one of them would rush in from the corral where he was shoeing a horse or branding calves and stir it up.

As time went on I learned much from the roundup cooks who were out for months on end with the chuck wagons, and could turn out a delicious meal from a covered iron pot over an open fire.

These hardy Western men were nearly all bachelors, and so cooked in self-defense, but they did know how. It was one of them, a grizzled old cowboy, who taught me that the tops of young beets, which I'd been throwing away, make the most delicious of all greens. So when I went home to West Virginia the following year I introduced my grandmother to beet greens. When she tried them she said: "Well! To think that I've been keeping house for forty years, and it took a man to teach me about the best greens there are—and a man in Montana at that!"

My clothes were so inappropriate, they were ridiculous, though I never thought so at the time. They were just the ordinary clothes of a girl living in West Virginia. Nothing new was bought for my trousseau but my traveling dress, which was dark blue camel's hair with a velvet jacket. For the rest I had a black silk, a dark blue one with tiers of ruffles on the skirt, and a white poplin trimmed with broad black velvet bands. They all had trains, and I trailed them around over my dirt floors, which became very dusty as the summer wore on. There was no canvas spread in the kitchen, and the dust just couldn't be kept down, though I sprinkled it, and swept it, and even scooped it up with a shovel. I did pin up my skirts to work in, and I wore aprons, but still, nothing more glaringly impractical can be imagined. I had brought one halfway sensible dress, a blue serge, but the first of May we had a twelve-inch fall of snow one night. The sun came out and it promptly melted; the dirt roof leaked, and a rivulet of yellow mud ran down into the improvised clothes closet in one corner of our room, ruining that particular dress. After that I just wore what I had until I wore them out.

People have asked me, and I have wondered myself, why I didn't send to Miles City for a few yards of calico and make some plain washable clothes. The truth is it never occurred to me. The day of mail order catalogues hadn't arrived, and we were not in the habit of sending for things. Then too I have come to the conclusion that I was simply not very bright.

I can point with pride to only one piece of practical common sense—the use I made of my wedding veil. I remembered how as a girl in West Virginia I had seen my cousin Betty's veil, which she had kept put away in a box. The folds of silk tulle had simply stuck together and torn, when we tried to pull them apart so we could wear the veil in a pageant. I'd resolved then that if I ever had a wedding veil, I shouldn't be so foolish, but should get some good out of it. So in Montana I cut chunks out of mine and put it in folds around my neck.

The veil kept me reasonably fresh-looking, but there was no such thing as cleaning fluid, and of course dry cleaning establishments were unknown. I've often thought how untidy we must have been. There were no coat hangers—we hung our clothes on a nail. I had brought no shoe polish, because I never thought of it. We didn't do anything to scuff shoes in the South. But after a few weeks of steady wear on a ranch my black kid buttoned boots were a sight.

One morning shortly before I went to my first roundup, some visitors arrived, among them Mr. Robinson, whose outfit was camped a few miles away, and who had ridden over to pay his respects to me. I saw the group of men ride up to the corral and dismount, and as I hurried to make myself presentable I wondered what to do about my shoes, which were shabby and foxy-red at the tips. Suddenly I remembered how as a child I had seen one of black Mammy's boys when getting ready to go to the village, turn up a black iron pot and take some of the soot to blacken his shoes. I seized a kettle and a rag and had just gotten the shabby spots covered when the visitors reached the house. I confessed what I had been doing and where I'd obtained my inspiration.

Mr. Robinson said: "Mrs. Alderson, you will get along all right on a cow ranch."

Such praise was music to me, because I was trying so hard, and my only woman neighbor gave me what would now be called an inferiority complex. She came to visit fairly often, either out of curiosity or to borrow something, and every time I saw her coming down the valley, riding side saddle on her awful old spike-tailed horse, her red mother hubbard showing up in the distance, cold chills would run up and down my spine. She had tried to sell me this horse for a saddle horse, thinking my husband would pay a big price for him because he was gentle. But as I was used to good horses he did not appeal to me at all, and I was foolish enough to say I didn't want him, instead of putting the burden on my husband. After that her opinion of me sank lower than ever.

But she continued to come, asking so many questions and offering so much advice as to the way my husband and Mr. Zook should run the ranch that we nicknamed her the "General Manager." Knowing we were well supplied with provisions for a long time ahead she was always offering to buy coffee, or a broom, or something, and we had to explain to her that the firm bought what it needed for its own use and could not sell. The broom became quite an issue between us. She found out somehow that we'd bought a dozen and she assured me that *anybody* with any sense could make a broom last a year. I'd already used up two in a few weeks. If she had been the kind of neighbor others were we'd have given her the broom or anything else that she needed. But we felt she had sized us up for silly young tenderfeet—me especially —and that she was simply trying to use us. What glorious news it was when we heard, in September, that the whole family was leaving the valley and going back to Idaho! Our nice bachelor neighbor, Jack Lynch, bought her shack and haystacks and little garden. There was nothing in the latter but green tomatoes, which he gave to me. I made them into pickles and gave him half.

Hardships, during these months, were far from being first in my thoughts. There was so much that wasn't hard. The ranch at Lame Deer was in a wide valley watered by a lovely little creek, between pine-studded hills. Our front door looked out upon a particularly symmetrical hill with one pine tree on it.

In later years after we had moved away, the site of our ranch was taken over by the Cheyenne Indian agency, and the little house where we spent our honeymoon became first the Indian interpreter's home and later his chicken house. Since then it has been torn down and quite a village has grown up on the spot, so much so that the last time I visited Lame Deer I couldn't locate the spot where our home had stood until I thought of sighting from the lone pine tree.

It was lovely that spring. The grass was long and thick after years of plentiful moisture, and the cattle were fat. The banks of Lame Deer Creek and farther down, of the Rosebud itself, were lined with the wild rose bushes which gave the Rosebud its name, and in June they were a mass of bloom—but Mother's letters showed very plainly she thought I had come to a wild, dreadful spot. She saw none of the things that lifted it up for me.

From time to time one of the boys would say hopefully: "I guess your mother'll be coming out to see you next summer, won't she, Mrs. Alderson?"—thinking how nice it would be for me if she came. I'd answer: "I can just see Mother out here. She thinks Montana's the jumping-off place."

I heard from her regularly and from Grandmother too, but both of them seemed to feel that they were writing to Mars. Grandmother wrote: "I fear that you will get sick or that the Indians will harm you, until I dream about it."

There were Indians all around us. Hardly a day passed that they didn't visit us and beg for food. Often the shack would grow suddenly dark, and I would look up, to see the blanketed form of an Indian blocking the window, shading his eyes with his robe to peer inside. It never dawned on me in that first year to be afraid of them, largely because I didn't know enough. Naively I thought them rather pathetic, with their dirt and their queer travesty of a white man's dress. How, I thought, could anyone fear such poor, miserable creatures? Yet these Indians were the Northern Cheyennes, known, until their surrender to General Miles a short two years before, as the deadliest of fighters and most implacable foes of the white man. As neighbors in the early Eighties, they were scarcely more comfortable than a powder magazine. But it took time before I realized this.

One of our steady visitors was old Chief Two Moons, who had played a leading part seven years before in chopping Custer's Command to pieces at the battle of the Little Big Horn. Now he was just an old beggar who came around to our house asking for coffee. He was absurd and squalid-looking, with his dirty cotton shirt turned wrong side out, and his white man's pants with the seat cut out, which he wore like a pair of leggings over a breech clout. Two

Moons' English was seemingly limited to "How,"
"Yes," and "No," but when he came for a meal he
would always ask in signs how many horses my husband would take for me. Once when Mr. Alderson
held up one finger, Two Moons laughed long and
loud, so we concluded that he had a sense of humor,
and that he asked the question more as flattery than
with a serious view to trade. Next time he asked for
my price in horses my husband began opening and
shutting both hands very rapidly. Two Moons
counted up to fifty or so and then said disgustedly:
"God damn, too many." It was his longest English
sentence.

The men of course knew the truth about our visitors, and I was never left alone at the ranch. No
matter how much work there was to be done one
man always had to stay with me. During the spring
this was simple enough, for the two men building
our house were always there, and then there was
our partner Mr. Zook. But we knew that Mr. Zook
was planning a trip to Chicago in the summer, when
the roundup would be keeping both Brown and Mr.
Alderson busy. And so, just when or how I don't
remember, we acquired a new member of the family,
Brown's brother, Hal Taliaferro, whose principal
duty was to stay at the ranch and guard me.

Chapter IV

Sometimes I wonder if too much hasn't been said about the grim aspects of frontier life. Later on in my marriage I came down to hard, bare facts; to loneliness and poverty. But that first spring and summer I was anything but lonely in spite of the lack of women. I had much to learn and hard work to do. But I had no children to look after, I lived in sur-

49

roundings of great beauty, I was happy in my marriage, and pioneering still seemed rather romantic.

We had plenty of visitors. Although the ranches were far apart—our near neighbors being five to ten miles distant—the men were always riding around looking for lost horses or moving stock, and as summer time approached, reps from miles away—even hundreds of miles—would come riding by on their way to join the roundup, and they would stop with us. A rep was a cowboy sent out by his outfit to represent them on some other part of the range, and gather up stray cattle bearing their brand. There were no fences, the cattle drifted for many miles, and these riders came to us from long distances—from the Belle Fourche in South Dakota, from Sun Dance on the edge of the Black Hills. Each would be traveling with a string of horses, his bed packed across the back of one. He would ride in, turn his horses in with ours, and stay for a meal or a night. If for the night, he would just throw his bed down out of doors. Later I heard that quite a joke was made on the roundup about the number of reps who found it necessary to pass by the Zook and Alderson ranch.

Once a week the mail came by horseback courier from Birney postoffice, twenty-five miles across the divide. Often it brought belated and unexpected wedding presents. The carrier was a young red-headed cowboy named Fred Banker, who spent the weekend with us, making the return trip to Birney on Monday. As he was a pleasant young fellow with a good singing voice, he was quite an addition to our musical evenings, and he and Johnny, Brown, and my husband, soon learned all the songs I knew on the guitar.

One week he brought a motherless colt he had picked up on the road over. Apparently the Sioux Indians, who were visiting the Cheyennes, had left it by accident, or because it was too weak to travel. When Freddie rode over the hill the appearance of extra bulk in the saddle occasioned some wonder at first. As he rode up he said: "There was no wedding present for you this mail, so I brought you this colt."

About the same time one of the bachelor neighbors brought me a motherless calf, also carried across his saddle, so I sent to Helena, the state capital, to have a brand recorded and thereupon entered the stock business. Our firm's brand was the sugar bowl and spoon; my individual brand was the first three letters of my maiden name with a bar underneath, TIF. The orphan stock that wore my brand was pretty pathetic, especially the calf. He was known as a "poddy," for feeding skimmed milk gave him a big stomach, and there was a sad look in his eyes, due to undernourishment. We called him Jack after the neighbor who brought him, and we kept him till he was a big five-year-old steer. He was what they called a "rough steer"—but he brought enough to buy a much-needed carpet to cover the splintery boards of my room. Those were later and harder times.

In 1883 we were all very young. Mr. Alderson was twenty-eight, and he was the oldest. I was twenty-three at the end of the summer; Johnny Zook and Hal were my age, Brown was a year younger. Our friends were in their twenties or early thirties. If we were empire builders we didn't feel like it or act the part. We made a game of everything, even the garden.

In April Mr. Alderson and Johnny and Brown took the plough and started breaking ground for a garden plot on a level space near the house. I shall never forget how tough the sod was; it didn't want to be ploughed. For longer than human memory the grass had grown and died and its roots had interlaced to form one of the strongest sods ever seen. Our little saddle horses weren't raised for such work, and besides they were only on grass, as we had no grain to give them, so they tired easily. The men could do just a few furrows at a time, and it took several days to make our small garden. But we planted it eventually with peas and lettuce and potatoes, and we turned the sod back over them, which was all we could do. We had fresh vegetables that summer, but the potatoes were quite flat.

While they were ploughing I would finish my housework—or just leave it unfinished, I'm afraid—and would go down there and watch them. When the horses had to rest the boys would come over and sit by me. Mr. Alderson was wearing a gold ring which became too tight as he worked, and he took it off and put it on my finger. A few days later it was gone.

We were working on the garden again when I noticed it was missing. I rushed back to the house and searched. I looked where the wash water had been thrown out, but the ring was nowhere. Brown had followed me up to the house to see what the matter was, and he now said soothingly:

"I'll bet Walt or some of them have hid that ring on you."

I said: "Go back down there and tell them I'm crying my eyes out"—but even that didn't produce the ring.

Next day I discovered a bruise on my forehead, and the moment I saw it I knew where the ring was. A few days before this the boys had taken the wagon and gone up into the hills to load pine poles for a fence. Of course I'd had to take my crocheting along and ride with them, perched on the running gears, and I'd sat under the pine trees and crocheted while they cut the poles. The gnats were thick on those warm spring days and in batting at them, as I now recalled, I had hit myself a crack over the eye with the ring.

I said to Brown: "I know where the ring is. It's up where you all were cutting poles."

He said: "You'll never find it. A magpie has got it by now."

But we saddled and rode up there, and I could see it gleaming in the pine needles before I got off my horse.

No, we were not very serious then. We didn't mind the hard things because we didn't expect them to last. Montana in the early Eighties was booming just like the stock market in 1929, and the same feverish optimism possessed all of us. I believe the same thing was true of many other frontier communities. Our little dirt-roofed shack didn't matter because our other house was building. And even the new house was to be only a stepping stone to something better. We didn't expect to live on a ranch all our lives—oh, my no! We used to talk and plan about where we would live when we were rich—we thought of St. Paul. It all looked so easy; the cows would have calves; and two years from now their calves would have calves, and we could figure it all out with a pencil and paper, how in no time at all we'd be cattle kings.

Well, it wasn't so. But there was a glamour to it while it lasted. Raising cattle never was like working on a farm. It was always uncertain and exciting— you had plenty of money or you were broke—and then, too, work on horseback, while dangerous and often very hard, wasn't drudgery. There was more freedom to it. Even we women felt that, though the freedom wasn't ours.

To me at first ranch life had endless novelty and fascination. There were horses to be broken and cattle to be branded, because new ones that we bought had to have our mark of ownership put on them before they were turned out on the range. Something was always going on in the corral, and I would leave the dishes standing in the kitchen and run down and watch, sometimes for hours. This having a Wild West show in one's own back yard was absorbing but it was terrifying; I never could get used to the sight, but would marvel how anyone could stay on such a wild, twisting, plunging mass of horseflesh. The boys took it all quite calmly, and would call to the rider to "Stay with him!" as though it were just a show. My husband always rode the ones that bucked the hardest. It was awful to see his head snap as if his neck would break, yet I never could stay away. However, Brown learned fast to be a good rider, and before long offered to take the worst ones, as he wasn't married.

Sometimes the boys would run races on their favorite horses, and I would hold the stakes. I often went riding when I ought to have been at work. I had a dark blue broadcloth riding habit, with a trailing skirt, and a tightly fitted coat made à la militaire, with three rows of brass buttons down the front. The buttons were a gift from a cousin who went to Annapolis, but was expelled along with two or three other Southern boys for hazing a negro midshipman. My riding habit was even more inappropriate to the surroundings than the rest of my clothes. But the men liked it, and there were no women around to criticize.

My mounts were a chapter in themselves. Gentle horses, as the term is understood in more civilized parts, were almost as rare in Montana as kangaroos. Therefore it was a routine operation, when I was going riding, for one of the boys to get on the horse first with my side saddle and skirt and "take the buck out of him," after which I would get on and ride off, trusting to Providence that he was through for the day. All cowboys, wherever they worked, had each his "string" of eight or ten horses, which actually belonged to the company but which were regarded as the sacred private property of the man who rode them. What was referred to as my "string" consisted of one elderly bay cow pony known as Old Pete. Old Pete was neither good-looking nor a lady's saddle horse, but he was considered gentle because he didn't buck except on starting out, and he would tolerate a side saddle. One day, however, Brown remarked with a thoughtful expression: "I'm afraid Old Pete's going to blow up with you some day when you're riding him. He did it with me."

If he did "blow up" I knew what would happen, but at the time it was Old Pete or nothing. When the roundup came, however, I acquired a new and safer mount.

Many young people have told me how they envied the freedom of the unfenced range as we knew it. But I fear that to the girls of today we should have seemed very quaint. Being married, I felt like a mother to the bachelors, even when they were older than I was, and none of them ever called me by my first name. As for Mr. Alderson, I never could bring myself to call him "Walt," the way the boys did. We didn't do that, in the South. Back home you would hear women say: "Why, I couldn't call my husband George"—or William or Henry. "You'd call a *servant* by his first name!" Of course I couldn't address my husband as I would a servant—not even in Montana where there were no servants! I believe we stuck all the more firmly to our principles of etiquette, because we were so far from civilization. We could still stand on ceremony, even though our floors were dirt.

I should add that in time Mr. Alderson took to calling me "Pardner," which became shortened to "Pardsy," and that after awhile I called him "Pardsy" too. So perhaps we were not so stiff after all. The boys were always scrupulous about swearing where I could hear them. But when they were working in the corral, they would forget that the wind could carry the sound up to the house. I caught nearly all of them that way at one time or another. Once I even caught Mr. Alderson. It was one day in the summer while they were finishing the new house. I had taken my darning and gone over there to sit, as I often did—because it was cooler there, and one of our new chairs, still done up in burlap, made a comfortable seat. A half-finished partition hid me from Mr. Alderson and Hal, who were working on the tongued-and-grooved ceiling. This was a difficult piece of work, and when Hal, in his irresponsible way, dropped his end of a board and tore out the whole groove, Mr. Alderson swore at him just terribly. I hated so to hear him, I dropped my work and ran to the shack—greatly to the delight of that scamp Hal.

Chapter V

In May Mr. Alderson left to go on the roundup, and for the second time in a few weeks I was minus a husband. This was to be the normal condition of affairs throughout my married life. The riding went on forever, but it was intensified in the summer and fall when they went on the roundup to brand the calves and gather the beef.

The old cattle range was divided up into districts,

each of which was worked by its own crew of men, with horses and wagons, under the command of a captain. The roundup to which my husband belonged started May 1 near Miles City and worked its way slowly up the Rosebud toward us, Mr. Alderson joining them after they were in our territory. He had his own cowboys and horses, but he did not take a wagon, as ours was accounted one of the smaller outfits in this section of the country, and our boys joined one of the other wagons.

On a beautiful Sunday morning in June they were camped only a few miles away, so I could ride over and pay them a visit. Mr. Zook, Hal and I started early. As we rode down into the valley of the Rosebud we saw a white patch—a wagon sheet stretched over the rear end of the chuck wagon. And from all sides the drives were coming in—cattle winding down from the hills, with riders following slowly on their flanks and at their rear, singing, calling or slapping their quirts against their chaps to make a noise; anything to keep the cattle moving. In the broad valley below were more cattle, thousands of them in one great herd, with more riders holding them, and over it all rose dust, and the noise of thousands of bawling throats. Men were at work in this big herd cutting out cows with calves into separate bunches, each according to the brand the mother wore. Mr. Alderson was in there cutting, and just as we rode up his

horse fell with him, but I didn't know it until somebody said to me: "He isn't hurt."

Dinner time was ten o'clock, but the men had been
up since before daybreak, and they were all hungry.
A few were left to hold the herd, while the rest rode
in, dismounted, and lined up before the cook's table
with their tin plates and cups in their hands. Some of
the company ate sitting on the ground. Others, myself among them, were enthroned on rolled-up cowboy beds, which made a perfect seat. My tin plate
was piled with good beefsteak, potatoes, baked beans
and stewed dried fruit; also canned tomatoes served
in a tin cup—I never ate any tomatoes that tasted
so good.

The cowboys talked to me with shy good manners,
explained things, and told me what to look for when
the afternoon riding began. A Mexican cowboy who
worked for one of the outfits was to ride his worst
horse, a noted outlaw. After dinner when they all
went to catch their fresh horses I fairly held my breath
while this horse was blindfolded and saddled. Greatly
to my surprise, and I think to the disappointment
of the rider, he trotted meekly off with never a buck.
Later on however he "blew up" in fine style, and
there was a great exhibition of riding.

Before I started home at the end of the afternoon
I met the foreman of one of the outfits, who told me
that he had a gentle horse. This horse was a beauti-

ful iron gray belonging to his boss, an Englishman, who wasn't using him at present.

"You might as well take him and ride him," said the foreman. "He's good and gentle and the boys are just spoiling him." So my side-saddle was transferred to Jerry, the iron gray, and I rode home that afternoon for the first time on a lady's mount.

Later on in the summer I again visited the roundup, even taking a little tent along and spending several nights and days. This was partly to release Hal, who would otherwise have had to stay at the ranch for my protection. I rode less than a modern girl would do, sleeping late in my tent instead of getting up at dawn and going on the long morning rides with the men, but when they came back with the cattle I would mount and help hold the herd. Toward the end of the summer my gray horse, Jerry, was reclaimed by his owner and I acquired a new mount, a gentle and beautifully gaited little mule. A man had ridden her into our ranch one day. He was a tall fellow and the mule was little. Every time he crossed Tongue River he had gotten his feet wet, and he wanted to trade for a good-sized horse. She was just the right size for me, so the trade was made, and I acquired as delightful a saddle animal as I ever sat upon. But when I appeared at the roundup riding a mule the boys made all manner of fun of me. I received so many offers of good horses to ride that day, that I really believe they were mortified on my behalf.

After the calf branding was finished there was a lull in midsummer when the roundup stopped working, and the men came home and put up hay. That kept them all busy for awhile, too busy to help me. For the first time in three months of married life I had to do all the work myself. And I felt horribly abused! When I had to dress my first chicken, I thought the end of the world had come. I didn't realize then that the spring, when we had all had such gay times together, was a slack season on the ranch, while haying time was one of the busiest of the whole year. I didn't realize how badly I'd been spoiled. I only knew that for the first time the wood box sometimes went unfilled. Instead of recognizing it for an oversight and saying, "Don't forget the wood," I brooded over it, waited until they were gone, carried the wood and water myself, and was sure my husband didn't love me. I needn't add that this was only a passing phase, and I soon came to my senses. I think many women are foolishly oversensitive in their first year of married life.

They had all warned me that if I ever heard a buzzing, whirring sound like the noise a locust makes on a hot day I should look out, for it was probably a rattlesnake. One warm afternoon I was resting on the mountain lion skin in front of the hearth, when

I heard a rustling among the pine boughs that filled the fireplace. Turning, I saw two great snakes coming out of the boughs and crawling over the hearth toward me. I was up and out of the house like a shot, calling my husband. He came and shot them both from the doorway—only to find they were harmless bull snakes. As bull snakes do no damage and are the enemy of rattlers, which they sometimes fight and kill, they are respected and let alone, and I felt rather foolish for raising the alarm. But my skin still crawled whenever I went near the fireplace, and I continued to think that snakes, no matter how mild their dispositions, are not ideal company around the house.

Shortly after this I was putting my rolls on the back of the stove to raise, when I heard that whirr I'd been warned about, right under my feet. As the boys had told me, it was unmistakable. I ran to the door shrieking, "Snakes, snakes!" The men were busy shingling the new house, and they came running. After my husband had shot the rattler, its writhing coils lay less than a foot from the print of my toe in the dust of the kitchen floor.

Next morning I went out to the stable to make an old hen finish setting. I had put her on the nest and placed a box over her, and I was reaching down in a dark corner for a rock to weight the box with, when I heard that whirr again. I had almost put my hand on another rattler.

For some time after that I was crawling all over. I saw snakes in every shadow; the fur rugs on the floor no longer invited me to stretch out. For the first time I understood the full meaning of the phrase "snakes in your boots"—although the snakes therein referred to were the kind that crawled out of a bottle. While I was still getting over the first snake scare, word came to Mr. Alderson that the furniture for our new house had arrived in Miles City and been freighted fifty miles up Tongue River to Liscom's ranch, where it was waiting for him to come and get it. I decided to go along, though the trip was to be made in a lumber wagon, and on this trip I met and talked to the first women I had seen, except for our unpleasant neighbor and her daughter, since leaving Miles City three months before. The first night we stopped at a ranch on Tongue River belonging to a retired Yankee sea captain, who had decided to better his fortune by raising cattle in the west. His three sons, two of whom I had met on the roundup, were all born at sea. Mrs. Howe was a pleasant middle-aged New England lady who won my ever-lasting gratitude by telling me how to bake a cake with one egg.

Next morning we left to get our furniture. Tongue River was "swimming," and the wagon could not cross that swift, muddy flood. So while I stayed another night with Mrs. Howe, Mr. Alderson and Brown built a raft to get the furniture and shingles across. Going home we took a different route to the Rosebud, and just as we reached the river something on the wagon broke.

My husband pointed down among the trees and said: "Pardsy, I think that's the Miller ranch and a woman lives there. Wouldn't you like to walk down?"

I did, and was well rewarded. For Mrs. Miller was a lovely young woman, with beautiful brown eyes and rosy cheeks. She had two children, a girl and a boy, and I believe she too was hungry to see one of her own sex. We spoke of each other as neighbors, though we knew we should see each other rarely, for thirty miles separated us. I was glad the accident to the wagon was serious enough to keep us there all night. The next night we reached home.

As we drove up Hal came out of the house, and his greeting startled us. It was: "My God, Walt, I'm glad to see you. I thought you were drowned."

It seems that while we were gone word came to the ranch, through a passing cowboy, that a man had been drowned in Tongue River the very day my husband was due to cross. Hal got on his horse and rode all night, crossing the divide, till he came to some people on Tongue River who told him that the victim was none of our party, but a stranger going towards Miles City. That act of solicitude was very like Hal, and helps to explain why we loved him.

All through that first year I had so many, many things to learn; washing, ironing, bread-making, the care of milk to make good butter; the care of fresh meat when an animal was butchered. I still dreaded washing above all other tasks.

I never learned to manage the hard water; my sheets and dish towels (the latter made of flour sacks) would never come white. And as I labored with aching back on wash day, I thought again of poor old Aunt Rose. She would beg us girls to hold up our skirts out of the dew, when we walked out in the evening, because they would be dampened just enough to catch the dust, and we would each have four or five of those many-ruffled petticoats in the wash every week. But when she asked us to hold them up and spare her that dreadfully hard work, we rejoined: "Why Auntie, you don't want us to expose our legs, do you?"

From the beginning I had dreamed of having a spring house, and the men built me a lovely one, fifty yards away from the kitchen. I soon found, however, that a spring house was one thing in the south, where there were any number of little colored children to send on errands, and quite a different thing in Montana, where I had to walk the fifty yards myself every time I wanted an egg or a piece of butter—and walk it again if I forgot anything, as I did frequently, you may be sure.

But I learned as fast as I could, and with a loyal and uncritical group of supporters to cheer me on, I soon built up an undeserved reputation as a wonderful cook. But I cooked for hungry men, and because a woman had prepared the food they thought it tasted better. Long years afterwards an elderly man would come up to me and say: "Oh, Mrs. Alderson, I've never forgotten a meal we had at your house—we'd just come in from fighting fire up in the hills, and I never ate a pie that tasted so good." And I'd remember the time he spoke of, and the tired men, grimy and red-eyed from days and nights of fighting a prairie fire that threatened to destroy miles of range, and I could not honestly claim credit for the pie.

In the wild plum season I put up preserves, gathering all I could of the tangy deliciously flavored fruit, and making use of such containers as I could find. One I remember was an old teapot with the spout broken off. Then too a neighbor had told me to saturate a string with coal oil, tie it around a bottle, set fire to the string, and when it burned off plunge the bottle into cold water. It worked very well. The bottle generally broke evenly all around, and when I had pasted cloth over the edge to make it safe, the result was satisfactory even though not beautiful to the eye.

One day at the end of the first summer my husband came to me with a gray blanket and said, "I wish you would make me a pair of pants out of this. My working pair won't last through the fall roundup, and I hate to spoil my good business suit."

At first I said No, believing that no woman knew how to make a man's clothes fit. But Mr. Alderson said I could rip up an old pair for a pattern, so I agreed to try. When they were done, one leg twisted a little below the knee.

"I will wear them tucked inside my boots and no one will know the difference," said my treasure of a husband.

Not only that, but he apparently bragged to every man on the roundup that I had made his trousers, casually giving out the impression that I was worth my weight in rubies at least. Soon cowboys began to come and beg me to "fox" their breeches "for any price you choose." This foxing was a way they had of re-inforcing store trousers for riding, a heart-shaped piece of buckskin being sewn to the seat and extended down the inside seams of the leg. The Indians usually tanned the buckskin a soft light brown, but when breeches were foxed with white buckskin the effect was startling, to say the least. After a few trials I became reasonably expert at sewing on the heavy stuff with a three-sided buckskin needle.

Chapter VI

WE MOVED INTO OUR NEW HOUSE IN AUGUST. IT had four rooms and was built of hewn logs seven inches square, so closely fitted together that they looked like a frame house. Old Uncle and Bill Baltimore stayed till the main work of construction was all done, and then Fred Banker, our mail-carrying cowboy, whose mail contract had expired by this time, came to do the finishing. Besides window and door frames he made me a built-in cupboard, with drawers and flour and sugar bins underneath, to take the place of the old chuck box which was my first kitchen cabinet. And wonder of wonders, the house had board floors, built double for warmth. My feet fairly flew over them. But the boards were covered with grease spots before long. Even water spotted that raw new pine.

Of the four rooms one was a bunk room for the boys and another was Johnny Zook's room. Across the hall were the kitchen and our bedroom. The walnut furniture, with its marble-topped dresser and wash stand, came all the way from St. Joe, Missouri, and was the gift of our partner, along with the bright carpet and curtains. There were a lounge, six small chairs and an easy chair, and book shelves with some of my father's books. On the walls, which were lined inside with muslin and papered with a flowered paper, hung two lovely etchings and old-fashioned oval portraits of Mr. Alderson's parents. My dear grandmother's silver candlesticks stood on the stone mantel. I cannot tell you what luxury all this represented in that place and time. There was no house like it anywhere in eastern Montana, outside of Miles City. And we never had one like it again.

Our bedroom with its huge fireplace, where we burned logs five feet long, was again the living room for all when the day's work was done. I never regretted the arrangement whereby we shared our home with our own nice cowboys, and with every stray rider who came our way. This was Mr. Alderson's idea; he had the highest ideals of home of any man I have ever known. Few families living in Montana had their cowboys live with them as we did. Nobody then thought of them as romantic. They were regarded as a wild and undesirable lot of citizens, but I always thought there was much injustice in this. Nice people in Miles City would as soon have thought of inviting a rattlesnake into their homes as a cowboy. The *only* places that made them welcome were the house of prostitution and the saloon. The wonder is that despite all that they kept their finer qualities intact.

Night after night we were all together in the bed-living room of the new house; the men would play cards, while I read or sewed. I was making baby clothes, but I held them so they wouldn't show. I did have fleeting moments in which I thought privacy in home life must be a wonderful thing. But in the main the friendliness of the arrangement more than made up for its drawbacks. I marveled at the boys' good manners—for few of them had had any advantages, and some could not read nor write. I wondered, too, at their neatness, since they had no women to wash for them but must keep clean through their own efforts.

In pride of appearance they were a contrast to

some of our eastern neighbors. We knew two young men, brothers, who had a cattle ranch on Hanging Woman Creek, near Tongue River. They came often to see us; their parents, I know, were fine people, for we saw their pictures. The father was head of a big import and export house in New York. These boys used to wear old dirty buckskin shirts which they never changed; they let their beards grow, and were in general as disreputable as they could make themselves. Just before they went home for a visit, they called on Mr. Alderson for a hair-cut—almost every ranch having an amateur barber in those days.

He said to them: "You're not going to go east in those clothes! You'll ruin the reputation of Montana." He wanted them to buy new in Miles City.

But they said: "Oh, no! If we go home like this, father will send us to the best tailor in New York to get clothes, and he'll pay for them."

So off they went as they were. When they got back they told us gleefully that their mother hadn't even let the maid pick up their old clothes to put them in the furnace; she made her use tongs. I shouldn't wonder but what those shirts were in even worse condition than they looked.

In a way you could not blame the people of Miles City for their opinion of cowboys, who were at their worst when they went to town. Their first idea was to get drunk and make a lot of noise; their next was to squander their money. That fall after the work was all done Brown went to Miles City, taking with him three hundred dollars in accumulated wages. When he came back a week or two later, all he had to show for his bank roll were a couple of new shirts, and a ring with an enormous purple glass stone in it, apparently meant to be taken for an amethyst.

There was one shirt of which he was particularly proud. It was of cream-colored flannel with a pinkish silk stripe woven into it. Never in all my life have I seen a garment shrink like Brown's "three-hundred-dollar shirt", as it was promptly named. You could fairly see it grow smaller; it shrank on him as he breathed; just the warmth of his body seemed to affect it. When it was soiled I offered to wash it for him, and did it as carefully as I could—but alas, Brown was never able to get into it again. He gave it to me for a blouse, and I wore it until it had shrunk too small for me. Later my first little girl wore it, and it never stopped shrinking, but went on getting smaller and thicker, until the day it was finally converted into a cleaning rag.

These men were my faithful guardians. Again and again I was all alone on the ranch with one of them. This was a commonplace of the times. The men *had* to be with the women for protection, and there was never a whisper of evil.

So complete was the faith of western men in the chivalry of their fellows, that one time when the boys all had to be away at once, they thought nothing of letting a perfect stranger, who had ridden in to look for a job, stay and look after me and my small baby. This happened later, when we were living on Tongue River. I accepted it as naturally as they did at the time, but in the light of after years and broader knowledge I now see in it something very American and very fine. I have often wondered whether the splendid comradely attitude of American men toward women did not originate in just such conditions as those of my early days in Montana.

There was a Mr. Young who kept a store and traded with the Indians at the mouth of Muddy Creek, up the Rosebud from our creek and about ten miles across country from us. We heard in the spring that he was planning to bring his family out from St. Paul to live in tents until he could build a house for them—the family consisting of a wife, sixteen-year-old daughter and six-year-old son. By this time, June or July, they were here and partly settled, and I was most anxious to meet them. So one Sunday afternoon I rode over with Brown to call, my husband being away.

Mrs. Young was a kind, motherly woman, and the daughter, Fanny, was attractive and full of life. I found her cleaning her jewelry, preparatory to putting it all away.

"I shall have no use for it here," she explained. "We see only Indians and half breeds."

I could have told her that she was wrong there; that her father's store was likely to be the busiest place in eastern Montana, as soon as word got around that he had a good-looking daughter. Beside his stock of Indian goods Mr. Young sold hats, gloves and tobacco to the cowboys. Knowing something of cowboys, I fully expected, and events showed I was right, that they would now wear out (or lose) more gloves than ever, and smoke themselves to death. Miss Young was the only unmarried lady within a radius of a hundred miles!

She and her mother insisted on our staying to an early supper, and when we started homewards in the June twilight Miss Young seemed delighted to ride a little way with us. Her father had told her that when she rode she must always have someone with her, because of the Indians about; her escort was usually one of the Rolands, a nice, respectable family of half breeds who lived near. This time there was no Roland boy, but she had forgotten all about that, and girl-like she rode and rode.

Finally, when we were halfway to our house, I said: "Brown, you'll have to go back with Miss Young, because she has ridden so far, I'm afraid her father will be angry with her."

Poor Brown, torn between conflicting claims of chivalry! He objected that then I should be left to ride on alone. But I insisted, pointing out that I knew the way, and that my horse was perfectly safe —since I was not riding Old Pete, but Jerry, the mount I had acquired at the roundup. Finally I overcame his protests, and he turned back with Miss Young.

When I rode up to our house Hal was looking out for us. His first words were: "Where's that brother of mine?"

When I told him he was furious, and explanations couldn't calm him. He said forcibly: "I'm going to teach that boy a lesson"—turned my horse out and hid the saddle, and told me to go to bed and keep quiet.

When Brown came riding in a couple of hours later I heard Hal ask him: "Where's Mrs. Alderson? Did she decide to stay all night?"

Brown nearly went crazy. But Hal stuck to his "lesson" through all the motions of getting ready to go on a search for me, till Brown caught sight of the gray buckskin seat of my side saddle where it was hanging up behind the house door.

The men who were left in charge of western women in those times took their trust very seriously. During all the years when I, and later my children, had to be watched over there were never but two slip-ups, and both occurred through some insistence of my own.

Of all my guardians Hal was the most amusing. I had had so many frights with snakes, that on summer nights when Mr. Alderson was on the roundup, Hal would take his bed—a roll of blankets done up in canvas—and put it down outside the door of the shack, saying soothingly, "Now if you get scared you can just holler, and old Sawney'll be right here." .He always referred to himself as "old Sawney"— why, I never knew, or can't remember.

He was a strange character, warm-hearted, reckless and wild. Considering the fateful part he played in our lives, it may be fitting to tell more about him. That summer, at a branding over on Tongue River, Hal had had words with an Indian; the Indian had used language which should, as they say, be spoken with a smile—and Hal had knocked him down off the high corral fence. The men all held their breath; with the Indians as they were then, someone could have been killed.

Until that happened our window shades had seemed a useless touch of civilization; why draw blinds when there was no one outside to look in, no one for miles and miles? But after the fracas Mr. Alderson cautioned me to draw them every night, especially when I was alone at the ranch with Hal. He feared the Indian would come riding by and take a shot at Hal through the lighted window.

On long, cold evenings when a big log burned in the fireplace and the coyotes howled outside, he would sit with me and talk. That was when he told me how he'd bragged on my riding to the boys at the roundup. He always brought in the kindling and logs for next morning's fire, and he depended on me to cross the hall and call him to get up.

One evening he said suddenly: "What'd you do if Old Sawney died some night? You'd go call me to get up, and there'd be Old Sawney dead. You'd be afraid of a dead person, wouldn't you?"

I said: "Goodness, Hal, don't talk like that!" But I couldn't hush him. I suppose something had started him to wondering how I should manage if I were left there alone, because he asked:

"What would you do? You couldn't go to the barn and saddle a horse for yourself, could you?"

And then he harked back to the picture of himself lying dead in the bunk room, which seemed to fascinate him, and he kept it up in this gruesome vein until finally I said:

"Hal, if you don't stop I'll tell Pardsy on you when he comes home."

He said: "Oh my God, don't tell Walt. I'll never hear the end of it."

And that settled that.

September was glorious. There was frost and sometimes ice at night, but the days were golden and full of sunshine. When the roundup was working near the ranch, Mr. Alderson and the boys would come home for visits, and I was still all too willing to stop my work and join in a piece of fun. One day I was washing in the kitchen and my husband was trying to help me, when Hal came in to say he had found a cow bogged down in the creek, and he wanted Mr. Alderson to go with him and help him.

Then he turned to me and said: "There's a nice patch of plums down there. Why don't you come and pick them while we're getting the cow out?"

That was enough for me. While they saddled my little mule and brought her to the door, I found a tin pail and a flour sack. I didn't stop to change into my riding habit, but went just as I was. I was wearing my dark blue silk, ruffled to the waist, with a pale blue cashmere jacket over it and a piece of my wedding veil folded into the collar. While the men went to the rescue of the poor old cow I started picking the plums; it was a beautiful patch and I was hungry for fresh fruit, besides wanting all I could get to make plum butter.

The bushes were high and thorny. I soon found that the biggest and reddest grew on the top branches, and I went after them recklessly. My skirt was soon torn beyond repair so I decided to help it, and as each ruffle snagged I would tear it all the way off and tie it around my waist, exposing great gaps of cotton sham underneath. By the time the boys came back with the cow I had all my plums. As I've said before, the boys were not proud of the fact that I rode a mule; they were always making fun of Susie, and when Hal now said that his horse could beat her home, I turned the plums over to my husband and said: "All right, I'll race you."

Away went Susie over brush and briar—for she really was faster than most of the horses on the ranch, and could jump so easily it was like sitting in a rocking chair. I soon lost my sombrero and every hairpin in my head, and arrived at our back door a sight. There I was with my hair streaming, my ruffles tied around my waist and the ones that were left scattered fitfully over my skirt; there in the middle of the kitchen floor was the wash tub just as I had left it— and there, talking to Johnny Zook, was Mr. John Holt from Miles City, one of the biggest cattlemen in the country, who had come out to buy our beef cattle. It was as embarrassing a moment as any I remember. But I won the race.

One other memory stands out of those months—

our dog. On his trip to Miles City in July Mr. Alderson had brought home a Newfoundland puppy—an adorable clumsy creature with enormous paws. By fall he had grown up to his paws and was the size of a small Shetland pony. We called him Major—and I have never known a dog so lovable or so smart. He learned faster than my children did later, and our whole household was soon teaching him tricks. Hal, perhaps with a view to avoiding work, taught him to carry wood for the stove and drop it one piece at a time into the wood box. When Mr. Alderson carried the bucket of warm skimmed milk to Jack, the motherless calf, he would give the empty pail to Major to carry back to the house, and I would open the kitchen door and take it from him and reward him with a lump of sugar.

Our boys had the cowboy habit of keeping their hats on in the house, so Mr. Alderson slyly trained Major to go round behind them when they were sitting at the table and remove their hats. One night about the middle of that winter an old trapper paid us a visit. He had come down off the mountains at the head of Lame Deer, where he had been trapping since fall and hadn't seen a soul. He brought a big bundle of beaver pelts with him, I remember, and he gave me the tails to make soup. Beaver-tail soup was considered a great delicacy. As the shaggy old fellow was warming his hands before the bedroom fire,

Major came along and decided to take off his hat. It was tied under his chin with a buckskin thong, but Major wouldn't give up, and I think for an instant the trapper thought his last moment had come.

Chapter VII

THE WEATHER GREW STEADILY COLDER AFTER
Thanksgiving, but the air was so rare and dry we were
not conscious of the change. So insidious was the
Montana cold that it was not deemed safe to be
without a thermometer, and the pathway to ours
was the best worn trail on the ranch. Almost the
first thing anyone said when he came in was: "Guess
how cold it is." It could be fifteen or twenty degrees
colder without one's realizing it, for usually the

colder it got the stiller the air was, and frozen ears and noses were not uncommon. Through the middle of the day the sunshine was glorious, but that dazzling brilliance was very hard on the eyes, often causing snow blindness and great pain. Not many had snow glasses in those days, so the boys would burn a piece of pitch pine and blacken the skin around their eyes and across their cheeks. I was quite startled when I first saw two men approaching with their faces so blackened, and was sure they were highwaymen. But later the only impression they made was on the towels. A pitch pine smudge is not easily removed.

Johnny Zook went home to St. Joe, Missouri, for the holidays, but we still had as many guests on the ranch as we could comfortably "sleep." One of them was a character already celebrated in the talk of our countryside. He was known as Packsaddle Jack.

This Packsaddle was a Texan, who had come up to Montana with a herd of cattle in eighteen eighty-one or two. Having made up his mind to stay north, he rode into a roundup camp to apply for a job. He was using an old-style Texas saddle, which was so worn out that the wooden tree showed through the leather in places, making it look, the boys said, like an old wooden packsaddle. The rickety old saddle, plus his cocky manner, caused a few grins to appear, and when he asked for a job with the outfit the wagon boss said he guessed he could hire him if he knew how to ride. Thereupon he had one of the boys rope an outlaw horse which none of them had ever ridden successfully. The newcomer threw his old worn-out saddle on the horse's back, and the animal almost bucked himself in two. But the saddle stayed together and the man stayed on; and from that time, in compliment to his ancient saddle and his magnificent ride, he was known as Packsaddle Jack.*

A famous rider and cowhand, he became the hero of every kind of tall story circulating on the range. In the legends he is boastful and dangerous, always pulling his gun and threatening somebody. The real Packsaddle who came to us that winter was a gray-haired man of uncertain age, who seldom carried a gun. He had been working for the OD outfit the previous summer, but when fall came and the round-up was over he was out of a job. About a third of the men in a round-up crew were usually kept on for the winter and the rest turned off, but Packsaddle was never one of those kept on the payroll; not that he wasn't a good hand, but he was always grumbling about the outfit he worked for, complaining of the food, and quarreling with the cook.

A typical Packsaddle story concerns a rainy morning in the roundup camp when the cook was struggling to get breakfast over an open camp fire. When Pack-

*In another version Packsaddle, when asked if he could ride, retorted: "I can ride anything this outfit's got on a packsaddle."

saddle came up to the fire to warm himself, the cook said: "Look out there, you'll upset my gravy." At that, they say, Jack jumped into the frying pan with boots and spurs, and kicked the fire to pieces.

As we knew him he was rather harmless, but he carried a chip on his shoulder, taking a superior attitude toward most of the people he met, and refusing to be friendly except with those he considered to "know sompin." The rest he dismissed as "pure scrubs." We had reason to feel flattered because, winter after winter, he came and made his home with us. His real name was Jack Morris. I'm sure I was the only person in all of Montana who called him "Mr. Morris," and I believe he rather liked it.

We celebrated the first Christmas in our new home with a party. One of the guests was Josh Sharp, a young lawyer from back east whose brother had a ranch on Tongue River. With Josh came a tall, gawky young fellow from New York. This young man had enjoyed every advantage of education and surroundings, but he had no social ease or natural graciousness, and I could not help contrasting him with the shy, friendly, courteous cowboys. Yet later, when we came to know him and he talked, he was so interesting; he had read and traveled, and knew so much that the rest of us didn't know.

Our other guests were Packsaddle Jack and our own boys. They were dressed up for the occasion in their best colored shirts and good trousers, and as always had a clean and attractive appearance. As for the absence of coats, that had long since ceased to trouble me.

I doubt if there was a turkey in Montana that Christmas, but we had oysters! We had persuaded a neighbor, coming from Miles City several days before Christmas, to bring us several cans of these, frozen, and packed in ice as a double precaution. I can make good eggnog and, with Christmas candies to supplement the eggnog, I hoped this dinner would be memorable for them all. I planned to serve it at three. The oysters, I hoped, would make an impression, as they were rarely seen out here on the frontier. For the pièce de résistance we had our own roast beef, than which no better could be found anywhere.

My table looked very Christmasy with a bowl in the center filled with pine cones and wild rose berries, that grow large and bright red here. On each side of the bowl were Grandmother's silver candlesticks (for I knew it would be getting candle-lighting time before our dinner was over) and a set of white doilies with border of red-edged wheels, and all the silver I owned—even the berry spoon, though there were no berries. The doilies did look pretty on the polished walnut table. I was really proud of myself as I took my seat at the head of the table, with the baking dish of scalloped oysters in front of me and the pretty

berry spoon to serve them with. What if my husband
did sit on the churn, turned upside down and covered
with a rug? What if I sat on a drygoods box, made
the right height by my father's copy of Shakespeare,
and William Cullen Bryant's "Gems of Prose and
Poetry"? The latter book had been given me by the
second of our mail-carrying cowboys, Mr. Miller,
when he left Montana. I never knew his background,
but he had a most gentlemanly appearance and the
book showed evidence of having been much read.
Finding it too bulky to carry on a horse, he had
wanted me to have it.

While my husband carved the beef roast I helped
everybody generously to oysters. I did not notice that
after the first exclamation of "think of oysters on a
cattle ranch in Montana," nothing was said.

When my husband finished serving and tasted the
oysters he said to me, "What's the matter with these
oysters?"

I fear some of the guests ate more than was wise,
just to spare my feelings. I needn't report on how
sick some of us were before morning, for the oysters
evidently had been tainted before they were frozen.
I could have cried of humiliation at my frustrated
effort to make this first Christmas a great success.
The men were very sympathetic. I think they feared
I'd boo-hoo, and kept saying "don't you care" and
praising the roast, the pie, and everything else. In

spite of the bad oysters, we did have a merry time before the disastrous effects began to appear.

At New Years Josh Sharp and the other boy were still with us, and Mrs. Young came over to visit, with Fanny and their six-year-old son. Our dog had never seen a child and was wild with joy. Every time anyone went out the dog pushed in; something he had never done before, and when shut out would paw on the window, with a look in his big brown eyes clearly indicating his desire for Charlie to come out and play.

One January night the dog barked so long and loud that my husband decided to go out, to see if a wolf or coyote could be nearby. He found two Indians in the angle of the house, slumped in their saddles and almost frozen. They were afraid of the dog and, in their stolid way, just sat there, not making a sound. They had started across the divide, but the snow was so deep their horses floundered till they were worn out, and I suppose the lights from our windows attracted them. Mr. Alderson brought them in by the fire and put their hands and feet into cold water. I got them a meal by the open fire in our room, as the kitchen fire was out. These Indians knew no English words to express themselves, but they drank the coffee and devoured huge helpings of steak. We put down a bed for them on the kitchen floor and gave their horses a feed of oats. In the morning they went on their way. I had heard it said that Indians never forget a kindness, and at that time I still believed it. Not long after we had a visit from some Sioux who had come to pow-wow with the Cheyennes. It was Sunday and we slept later than usual. When we raised the window curtains on a beautiful, brilliant morning the earth seemed covered with Indians. They were swarming all over the white valley and into our dooryard. Hal had gotten up ahead of us to light the fire, and when I went into the kitchen to help get breakfast I found him talking to a young, well-educated squaw called Mary. He told me later that when she came in he had pointed to my room and said: "White Squaw in there," and that Mary had replied: "Why do you say White Squaw? Why don't you say White Woman?"

This Mary, who was acting as interpreter for the head chiefs, said: "We don't expect you to feed a crowd but will appreciate it if you will give the chiefs and their interpreter breakfast."

When we consented, Mary went out and harangued with the rest of the crowd and sent them on their way. One of those we fed was the noted Sioux chief "Young-Man-Afraid-of-His-Horses." He was old and undersized, yet his bearing was dignified and he looked very much a chief. Another chief, "White Eagle," was one of the finest-looking Indians I have ever seen. They seemed to have only one English word to express relationship, the word "sister," and Mary seemed sister to them all.

After they had eaten and sat smoking and talking among themselves, Mary turned to me and said: "The chiefs want to give you something they have on, in appreciation of the meal and your kindness." I told her I would like a lock of hair of each chief. They kept talking among themselves.

Mary turned again to me and said: "They are superstitious about cutting their hair for a white person."

I said, "Tell them we do not want pay for their breakfast."

Finally, as a great favor, Young-Man-Afraid-of-His-Horses pulled his braided hair to the front, singled out a wisp of, I'm sure, not over a dozen hairs, and asked Mary to cut it off and give it to me. I had to be content and was profuse in my thanks. I carefully divided it later, to send to two of my Sunday School girls in West Virginia who were collecting locks of hair of notable people. They would now have an Indian chief's—to keep beside one of Patrick Henry's!

Meanwhile the cold kept getting more intense, until in February the temperature hovered around 30 below zero. The snow drifted deep in places on the divide between the two rivers, so that going for the mail was real work, but it packed down on the roads, and the sleighing was splendid. My husband put runners on the spring wagon and built a bob for hauling wood and fence posts. The stockmen were already beginning to talk fences and preparing to build them. I hated to think of barbed wire coming in, because I had already acquired the love of an unfenced country, but the men said it was bound to come.

I was busy packing up for a stay of a month or six weeks in Miles City, putting my grandmother's silver away in the bureau drawers, because the boys insisted they were afraid to use it. I hated to leave the dog, he was so human and so devoted to us. But it was a pleasure to look forward to his joy on our return. He had shown when little Charlie came to visit how fond he was of children, and we would be bringing a baby back with us.

Of all the little household gods which meant so much in that remote country, I took only one with me, the small Confederate flag, which had been my father's. I took that only by accident, because it had never been out of my trunk. I said farewell to the house on a dazzling, frosty morning. It was still thirty below. But I had on Johnny Zook's buffalo coat which he had left for me—it weighed a ton, and it made me look like a fat brown bear, but it was impenetrable to cold. I had his sealskin cap, and a beautiful pair of sealskin gloves lined with wool which he had sent me for Christmas from St. Louis, and a big heated log in the bottom of the sleigh which had been warmed all night by the fire, and warm fur robes around me. I didn't know it was cold.

On the way in we stopped overnight at a road ranch where all the guests had to sleep in one room, with just curtains between the beds. There was one other couple stopping there besides ourselves, and the women went to bed first.

When Mr. Alderson came in it was dark, and he called out in a loud whisper: "Where are you?"

I had a good notion not to answer him, but relented. I remember I went to sleep thinking "Wouldn't mother think this was dreadful?"

Chapter VIII

MILES CITY WAS SOMETHING OF A PROBLEM, AS
there were no hospitals and no nurses. However, I
knew one woman who lived there; I had met her
on the train, coming out here from St. Paul, so when
I knew I was to go to Miles City I wrote and asked
her to find a place for me. She wrote back that no
one was willing to take a woman in that condition.
"But," she added "my mother was a midwife and I

know a good deal about nursing." And she went on to say that she would take me if I didn't object to the small back bedroom which was all they had. She and her husband would sleep on a couch in the sitting room, but she would have to share my closet in the bedroom as it was the only one.

At the time this sounded like the best arrangement we could make and it doubtless was, but it had many flaws. Because of the closet arrangement there was a good deal of going out and in, and very little privacy. Later the landlady was very little help with the baby. I don't think she was the type to care for nursing.

As it was the slack season at the ranch, my husband was able to be with me most of the time. I had about three weeks to wait before the baby was born in March. This interval passed with only one incident. Ice would gorge in the Yellowstone River every spring, and for years Miles City was subject to floods. While I was staying in this woman's house, one of these floods threatened, and early one morning I, my trunk and the baby clothes were packed into a wagon and taken to the Macqueen House, which was on higher ground. I was given a room directly over the bar, and I remember thinking it would be just my luck to have the baby come while I was in that old tissue-paper hotel. But the gorge broke or was blown up, and I got back to the little house in time. I remember that after this happened great chunks of ice lay in Main Street for weeks.

The doctor was a nice old Kentuckian, and I fared, I suppose, as well as the average young mother. Then, when we had had barely two days in which to rejoice over the birth of our baby girl, a telegram came, addressed to Mr. Alderson. He had gone up to town, and the landlady brought it to me. I thought it was a wire of congratulation from his brother-in-law in Kansas, and asked her to read it.

It said: "Indians have burned your house. Come immediately with sheriff and posse."

It seemed ages before a messenger located my husband and he returned, accompanied by the doctor who said, "Your husband has been deputized and it is very necessary that he go and see about this, but if you are going to worry yourself sick over it he won't go."

I said that of course he must go. During that long afternoon I listened to repeated warnings about the bad effect my worrying and grieving might have on the baby, and I gave myself many a mental shake and tried to think of our loss as one only of material things. But I never can forget the four days and nights, especially the nights, that I lay in that small back room wondering why the Indians had turned against us, what was happening, and if there would be an Indian outbreak and my husband would be killed.

Again it was men who gave unstintingly of their sympathy. Our landlord was working on the new courthouse, and he would come in and tell me every rumor he heard. An old saloon keeper sent me two bottles of champagne, and a message saying how "sorry he was to hear our nice home was burned." The proprietor of the hotel sent me flowers. I had heard that the latter often "painted the town red," but at the moment, had I been President, I would have given him a Cabinet position. During these endless days while I waited for my husband's return no woman outside of the landlady came to see me or offered her sympathy. If one had come, I would have been so glad to see her, I believe I would have kissed her feet.

My husband returned at last to report that the house was a total loss, that the Indians had surrendered, but that he had found nothing of any value belonging to us in the tepees he had searched, that the ashes of the house had been sifted but my Grandmother's silver was not recovered. Bad as all this was, the worst was learning that the Indians had shot our dog out of pure meanness—shot him so full of holes that the boys couldn't even save his beautiful furry hide.

This disaster had come upon us through Hal's fault. Here was how it had happened.

The northern Cheyennes, now that the buffalo were all gone, were poor, wandering from river to river visiting their kin, begging and maybe killing a beef now and then. A lodge consisted of a chief's or sub-chief's relatives and his squaw's relatives, which made a big family. An Indian sub-chief named Black Wolf, living on a tributary to Tongue River across the divide from us, had brought his lodge to visit on the Rosebud not far from our ranch. On a day of melting snow, he had come round begging for food and tobacco; the boys fed him, and afterwards he sat down to smoke on a pile of fence posts, some yards from our door. There was a man named Reinhart who had been working for us the latter part of the winter, getting out poles for the fences. When Hal looked out the door and saw the Indian sunning himself, he said to Reinhart:

"I'll bet you five dollars I can put a hole through that old Indian's hat without touching his head."

The other man of course replied: "I'll bet you can't."

Hal drew his six shooter and fired, just nicking the Indian's scalp. Black Wolf of course was furious; he could not and would not believe that Hal had not meant to kill him. When they found they could not pacify him they let him go, and rode hurriedly to

Young's store ten miles away to get help in defending
the property, for they knew what was coming. They
got three or four cowboys and some arms, but Mr.
Young was so sure there would be an uprising, he
wouldn't let his guns go. They had intended to get
inside the house and hold it, but when they got back
after several hours they were too late; the Indians,
the whole lodge, were in possession. Squaws and
papooses were seated in a semi-circle in the front
yard, while the bucks were carrying out bureau
drawers and emptying the contents in the midst of
them for them to help themselves, afterwards tossing
the empty drawers against the side of the house. Hal,
realizing that they meant to set fire to it, rode up to
them as near as he dared, promising them beef, coffee,
ponies and tobacco. But when they started shooting
at him, tearing up the earth under his horse, he
realized it was no use, and the men could do nothing
but ride up on top of a hill and watch while the
house roared into flames. It was chinked with oakum
between the logs, which made it burn all the faster.

This was Tuesday, March 18th, the day the baby
was born. Distances were great and travel difficult,
and it was not until Sunday morning that the sheriff
and posse from Miles City, with many settlers and
cowboys, had the Indians surrounded on the Rosebud and persuaded them to stack their arms and
surrender. Afterwards my husband went with the

interpreter through the tepees. He found Black Wolf reposing on one of my feather pillows, a red cord from off my best pin cushion around his hat. Hal's bullet had done him no harm. The Indians had camped by our house from Tuesday till Saturday, had eaten a year's supply of groceries, ten deer hams I was curing for summer use and all our chickens, besides burning the corral posts and poles, and cutting up the saddles.

The silver, as I say, was never found, and I feel sure that the Indians divided it among themselves and maybe beat it into bracelets and other jewelry. This same silver that I lost in the fire had been through a fire before, when my grandmother's home in Union was burned to the ground before the Civil War. She and the children barely escaped with their lives, but every piece of silver had been counted and put away the night before the fire as it was every night in good old Southern fashion, locked in a cabinet; and afterwards the ashes were taken up and sifted and the melted bullion recovered, and she and my grandfather took it to Philadelphia, and had it made over into spoons which I brought out to Montana and lost.

The boys had heard me tell this story, so after the Indians' surrender they sifted the ashes of our house but found nothing, only the plated ware, twisted and burned in the ashes where the kitchen cupboard had stood. They said that where the bedroom had been they found the marble top of the bureau lying, perfectly intact or so it seemed; but when they touched it, it turned to powder.

Indeed I tried not to whine over our misfortune, but fear I did so sometimes through weakness of the flesh. Such losses are not felt all at once, but repeatedly as each separate object is missed, things valued not only for themselves but for reasons of friendship as well. About the time the new house was finished Brown had sent east for a most elaborate wash-stand set of flowered cream-colored china with gilt edges and there were a hundred other things, little and big, which we never had money to replace. Many years afterwards my son was running cattle near the Cheyenne reservation, and he hired a Cheyenne Indian one summer to help him put up hay. At the table one day this Cheyenne said:

"Are you the son of the woman whose house was burned?"

Walter said he was.

The Indian went on: "I was a papoose then. My mother gave me a spoon like this to play with. It might be around the tepee yet."

Walter said: "I will give you almost anything if you bring that spoon." But the Indian never came back.

That spring of 1884 the government acted

promptly and impartially against the offenders on both sides. The two Indians who set fire to the house confessed at the trial and were sent to the penitentiary. Hal was wanted not only by the civil authorities but by the Indian Bureau, and he left the country a fugitive from justice—riding my husband's best cutting horse! Miss Young and her mother, our neighbors on Muddy Creek, blackened his light hair and mustache with shoe polish and he got away, even riding some miles with the stock inspector who was trying to find him. I have heard it said that just before he left Montana he was hiding at the LX Bar ranch on Powder River, when somebody came and told him that the Deputy U. S. Marshal was in sight, riding down the long fenced lane that led to the house. Hal waited until the Marshal was almost up to him; then took his horse and rode to the bank of Powder River, which was in flood and a mass of floating, grinding cakes of ice. While the officers watched he plunged his horse into the stream and swam to the other side, knowing well that no one would dare to follow. On the other bank he stopped and unsaddled, wrung out his saddle blanket and waved it at his pursuers in a final Hal-like gesture; then saddled again and rode away. That, at any rate, is the story. I don't know whether it's true or not, but it sounds just like Hal.

We heard that he went to Texas, and for years

after that we lost track of him. But he wound up eventually in Kansas, where he married and became a prosperous farmer.

Hal was to me the puzzling feature of the whole affair. People who knew him in later years said he never once seemed to realize the trouble he had caused us, but would laugh and joke about all that had happened. Yet he was fond of us, too, for in his wild way he was quite determined to ride into Miles City to see me and the baby before he left the country, and it was all his friends could do to prevent his taking the risk. His brothers always said that he never thought before he did a thing. And I don't believe he ever thought after.

Chapter IX

THERE WAS ONLY ONE COURSE POSSIBLE AFTER THE
fire, and that was for me to stay in Miles City until
a new home was ready. This would be a matter of
many months, so instead of staying at the hotel with
the baby all that time I joined forces with a young
woman from Iowa, who was married to a cattleman
friend of my husband's. She had a baby just two
weeks older than mine, and her husband, like mine.

was away a great deal. This couple had taken a small frame house, and it was decided that the baby and I move in with them and share expenses.

While this arrangement had much to recommend it, there were drawbacks. The young woman and I were not very congenial, as she was from Iowa, and had strict ideas. She regarded me as an object of pity because my husband sometimes went into a saloon with other men and took a drink. She could not understand my unconcern at this behavior, and I remember once she remarked in a superior tone: "Oh, well, you come from the South, where all men drink." Her greatest pride was that her own husband didn't drink or smoke, and when, one night while I was staying with her, he came home smoking a cigar and smelling of liquor, she cried and carried on all night.

I don't think my being there helped matters any, because she had made such a fuss a short time before this when I received a visit from a nice old German saloon keeper, the one who had sent me two bottles of champagne when the baby was born. He called one afternoon to see the baby, and the Iowa lady ran out into the yard when she saw him coming, so she wouldn't have to meet him. Her own baby meanwhile was howling on the bed where she had put him down, but she wouldn't come back into the house while the saloon man was there.

This would have seemed silly to me anywhere, but seemed particularly so in Montana at that time. The West was very tolerant toward the lesser faults of human conduct. It was even willing to overlook the greater if they were not repeated. A man's past was not questioned, nor a woman's either; the present was what counted. A man could even be known as wanted by the law elsewhere, yet this was not held against him here so long as he showed a willingness to walk the straight path. Half the charm of the country for me was its broad-mindedness. I loved it from the first.

I hadn't needed to come to Montana to find out that a new country offered greater personal liberty than an old and settled one. I had learned this while visiting my aunt in Kansas, and it was one of the reasons why I so enjoyed my visits there. I always thought that people should be judged for their human qualities alone. However, I didn't like everybody I met out here by any means. I was struck by the number of people who thought it necessary to apologize for being in the West. With the first breath they would explain that they were, of course, out here for their health, and with the next they would tell you all about *who* they were, and how rich and important and aristocratic their connections were back East. I never had any patience with that kind of thing. I've always said there were two things you never needed to talk about—your blue blood and your religion; if you had a speck of either, it was bound to show in some other way.

The case of the Iowa lady went to show that you never can tell about people. Not more than a year after she made that fuss over her husband taking a drink, he died. And what did she do but marry an old Texan, who had the reputation of being the most profane man in the country except Packsaddle Jack, and who was one of the hardest smokers and drinkers I ever knew.

While I was staying in Miles City, my husband and the boys were moving our outfit and building a house on Tongue River, thirty miles east across the divide from our old home. Mr. Alderson and Mr. Zook had decided not to stay on Lame Deer. The snow fell deep there in winter, and with the house gone there was nothing to hold any of us, since no one took up land in those days. So they moved, and because of moving they ran head-on, a second time, into near-disaster with the Cheyennes. And for the second time it was no fault of their own.

All that spring the boys were working hard locating our cattle on the new range. The cows had to be driven to water until they learned where it was; then, if they had their calves on the new range, they would stay. All this required extra help, and Packsaddle Jack was now with the firm.

The Cheyennes were all around the new location, as they had been around the old, and the place where Packsaddle drove his herd to water was not far from the tepee of an Indian named Iron Shirt. Every day, when he passed by with the cattle, Iron Shirt would come out with his dogs and try to stampede them. Packsaddle remonstrated, and told the Indian that if he persisted in stampeding the cattle, he'd shoot his dogs, or him. A few mornings later, when Iron Shirt came out of his tepee, urged the dogs on to stampede the cattle, and waved his blanket at them besides, Jack shot him and broke his arm.

I am thankful to say I knew nothing of this until it was over. The shot was fired in the early morning before breakfast. Jack rode back at once to report to Mr. Alderson. Once more, an Indian uprising stared us in the face. In an incredibly short time, they said, the bluff across the river was thick with the black silhouettes of mounted Indians.

My husband rode five miles up the river to Mr. Brewster, the nearest white neighbor, to warn him and get help. He thought they might gather at our ranch and stand off an attack, as the partly completed house, which was now seven logs high, would make a good fort. The men drove the saddle horses inside and got ready.

Due to the marvelous Indian system of signaling, all the Cheyennes in Montana seemed to know of the shooting, and they rode up and down the opposite river bluff all day. But when daylight next morning came and passed and no attack materialized, everyone felt that the crisis was over. Mr. Alderson persuaded Packsaddle that he must go into Miles City and give himself up. My husband then rode down to Iron Shirt's tepee and set his arm. He also made him a big present of coffee, sugar and beef.

Iron Shirt reacted to this kindness in the most grateful manner. He became much attached to Mr. Alderson, and would come up every day to where the house was being built, following him everywhere with seemingly dog-like devotion. However, as he was a stolid Indian and rarely said anything, and as he always carried a gun, some of the men began to wonder whether he was really as devoted to Mr. Alderson as he seemed, or was merely looking for a chance to kill him. Mr. Alderson persuaded him to leave his gun aside, and after that everyone breathed easier. Jack was acquitted, but on the advice of all concerned he found work on another range for the time being.

Before the Iron Shirt incident occurred, I had given up all attempt at joint housekeeping and moved back to the hotel. My principal occupation for weeks was shortening baby clothes. The people at the hotel were kindness itself, and after a new misfortune came upon us they were more solicitous than ever for the baby and me. But I suffered a good deal from the monotony and the lack of fresh air and exercise. For us, in our straitened circumstances, a baby carriage was out of the question. When I went out I had to carry our healthy four-months-old, and she seemed to gain in weight with every step I took, so long walks were impossible.

One evening when I was getting the baby ready for bed, the landlord's sister came in, and taking the baby from my arms said, "Someone in the parlor wants to see you. Get ready as soon as you can and I'll take the baby."

When I had straightened my dress and hair, I followed her to the public parlor to find it full of men. Many I knew only by sight, but recognized as stockmen who came and went around Miles City. And there in the middle of them was my baby, sitting in as nice a baby carriage as I have ever seen, cooing happily at her admirers. I was ready to cry, as extreme kindness always affects me in this way. I was saved by the spokesman, who came to the rescue with a witty remark which I now can't remember. He gave me a paper with all their names on it, and then he said something about their seeing me carry the baby out, and their all knowing and admiring my husband, and their sympathy for the ill luck which had come to our door. Is it any wonder that I was overcome, or that I thought and still think that this rough new country beat any civilized place I had ever known for kindness of heart? They were all homeless men, or at least far from home ties. Perhaps that quickened their sympathy. I have thought since how pleased those kindly gentlemen would be to know that their baby buggy served all my four children, and was afterwards handed down to a neighbor.

I had two more rather unusual experiences in Miles City. The first one was not without its humor. After all I have said in praise of broad-mindedness, it may well appear that the joke was on me.

Once a week during that summer I stayed at the Macqueen House, I would take the baby into the hotel parlor for the morning, while the chambermaid gave my room a thorough cleaning. One morning when I had moved in there with my sewing—I was shortening baby clothes, as usual—a dark-haired, dark-eyed young woman came into the room. She was striking in appearance and smartly dressed. I had seen her before, and knew she was staying at the hotel, but had never had occasion to speak to her. She got down on her knees and began making a fuss over the baby, who was of course delighted. Then she started talking to me. She told me she was waiting for her husband, who was on his way up the trail from Texas with cattle. She didn't know how much longer she would have to wait, and she was so lonely.

I could sympathize. I was lonely too. I offered her books; she said she had plenty to read.

Then I said, rather hesitantly: "I take the baby out every afternoon in her carriage. It is not very thrilling, but if you would care to go with us—"

Well, she jumped at the offer.

So a day or two after that, when the baby and I were getting ready to go for our walk, I went and knocked at the door of her room to invite her to come with us. A voice said: "Come in." I opened the door—and there she stood in front of her bureau, with hardly more than a stitch of clothing on; just a little chemise. She was pinning on her hat. I must confess that I was taken aback, though I could not help noticing that she had a very pretty figure. I asked her if she cared to go walking. She explained that she had another engagement. Although my mind did not work very quickly, it did seem strange to me at the time that she should say "Come in" like that, when she could not know who was knocking at the door. It might have been anybody!

Very shortly afterwards I learned, from the hotel proprietor's sister, that she was one of the most notorious women in the West at that time. The facts had only just come out. This woman—her name was

Connie—had had a habit of going out on the hotel porch after dinner, and talking with the men, and one day while she was sitting there the madam of a house of ill fame in the city had come by and recognized her, and had told the hotel proprietor. She was asked to leave the hotel at once, and her protector also. A wealthy stockman had been keeping her there, but she had been so quiet that no one suspected anything. Even looking back, I could see only one thing that could be questioned in her conduct; she would go down to breakfast in the hotel wearing a very beautiful satin mother hubbard, hand-painted with flowers, which was hardly appropriate for a public dining room.

To think that I was only saved from walking out on the public streets with her by the fact that she had another engagement—! However, it is possible that she was not wholly sincere in her desire to go walking with the baby and me. I think she simply enjoyed fooling me. I believe she thought: "This is a silly little thing, and I am smarter than she is, and I can pull the wool over her eyes."

We heard later that she went straight back to the red light district. But she did not stay there long. There was a wealthy Englishman, among several such around Miles City at that time, whose brother later came into a title; and this man set her up in an establishment of her own with horses, carriage, everything, and was seen with her everywhere. She would even appear at the races—for the town boasted a race track in those days—dressed in his cream and scarlet colors. It was a most brazen performance, and scandalized even Miles City. One day at the height of her notoriety I was right next to her carriage, but we never spoke as we passed by.

The other experience which stood out at this time was of a very different order. One morning the chambermaid told me that a cowboy was dying in a room downstairs. He had come up the trail from Texas, and had been shot, in a barroom quarrel, by the colored cook of an outfit both worked for. Knowing how scarce women were in Miles City, and thinking that the presence of one might be some comfort to the dying boy, I asked the maid to stay with the baby, and went down to him. The room was full of men standing around his bed. I took his hand and said: "I'm so sorry"—which was all I could say. He had a striking face, with dark blue eyes which never left mine until the doctor closed them. He did not seem to be in great pain. They said he had been shot in the stomach, and his breath just kept coming a little shorter and quicker until he died. It was hard to free my hand from his, which had closed over mine so tightly that the wedding ring cut in.

I never heard much more about this tragic affair,

but I do not believe the cowboy was blameless. They said he had been harsh in his treatment of the Negro. I know that no move was ever made to bring the latter to justice. Those young men who traveled north with the herds were far from home and all gentling influences, and they were prone to commit rash and violent acts. It was a pity, and in the case of a young man like this one a great waste as well. For there was great good in these wild and homeless boys, as no one knew better than I.

Chapter X

Aᴛᴇʀ ᴍʏ ʜᴜsʙᴀɴᴅ sʜɪᴘᴘᴇᴅ ʜɪs ʙᴇᴇꜰ ɪɴ Aᴜɢᴜsᴛ he brought the baby and me to our new home on Tongue River. Again it was a hundred-mile trip from Miles City, and the baby and I had been out of the hotel so little that our faces blistered the first half day, though I carried an umbrella. We stopped at a new road ranch where a kindly woman gave us fresh cream to relieve the sunburn. She also furnished material and helped me make a dark blue sunbonnet for the baby, lined with white paper around the face. All in all she was so nice and kind and clean, I didn't care if people did say she wasn't married to the man of the place.

The men had built our new house on high ground above the river, where there were no trees. It looked bleak to me after our lovely, sheltered valley of the Lame Deer, and of course I wanted to know why they hadn't built among the cottonwoods on the river bottom. I was told that it was because of cloudbursts, which occasionally sent floods sweeping down the riverbeds in this rough country. One afternoon a year or two later there were thunderheads above the Wolf Mountains, so big and black that a man who was staying with us remarked: "I shouldn't wonder if we hear of a cloudburst tomorrow." He had hardly finished speaking when a wall of water swept down a tributary which we called Zook Creek, right beside the house. It came boiling along at fearful speed, great trees bouncing on its crest, and I'll never forget the stench of mud and decay which rose from it. One of the boys jumped on his horse bareback and galloped out to cut the stake ropes of two or three of our saddle horses, which were picketed in the creek bottom right in the path of the flood.

The men liked the new location because the hay bottoms were very much bigger than they were in

Lame Deer valley. I was already learning to keep my feelings to myself.

The house was larger than the one on Lame Deer since it had two stories, but in other ways there was no comparison. Inside we had a set of cheap yellow oak furniture, which I had bought when I moved in with the Iowa lady, and little else. The upstairs part was never finished, but we furnished it with beds, and when we had women visitors we put them up there—the bachelors going in the bunk room with the boys. I always loved to listen to rain on a roof. It had a beautiful sound, drumming on the shingles above our second story. When a rainy day came I would think, after putting the baby down for her nap: "Oh, if I could only take a book and go up there and lie and listen to the rain." I never once did it.

In many ways life was harder now. The men still helped—it wasn't that. After each meal they would play a game of pitch to see who would do the dishes —including the company, if any were present—and I never had to do them myself. But the work was unending, just the same. I don't doubt that I was overconscientious. Much as I hated to wash and iron, I should never have ventured to take a short cut without the moral backing of another woman. Fortunately I found in a magazine a letter of housekeeping hints written by an English woman who had lived on a ranch. She said: "Only iron one or two of the baby's best dresses to keep for special occasions. Fold the others and put them away without ironing; then, when baby soils a dress, the dread of the hard work of ironing does not incline you to let her go dirty." That seemed to me very sensible, as did her advice not to iron sheets and pillow cases. She said that without ironing they smelled sweeter, which was true—a wonderful excuse, upon which I gladly seized.

There were more women in the country now, but I didn't see much of them. The men did the traveling around; the women seldom left the ranch. Distances compared with those of today were unbelievably great; we were only thirty-five miles from our good friends the Youngs after we moved to Tongue River, but those thirty-five miles of winding river bottom and high, grassy divide were like a Chinese wall dividing us, and we saw each other only twice a year. Ten miles down the river the foreman of the SH ranch had a wife, but I didn't see her either. I was told she thought I was stuck up because I didn't buy her butter at eighty-five cents a pound!

About the only woman I did see with any regularity was the mail carrier's wife. The government had changed the route, and mail now came to us over the hills from Sheridan, Wyoming. It was a terribly rough two-day trip of sixty miles, but the carrier's wife made it with him in the spring wagon, because she had lost her little girl, and even that difficult journey was better than staying home alone. She and her husband usually spent the night with us, and she gave me some housekeeping hints. But in the main I had to depend on men for both companionship and advice.

They were invariably interested and willing, but their counsel was not always reliable. For instance; the wild onion was the first green thing to come up in the spring; the cows ate it, and milk became so tainted that we weren't able to drink it. So I asked an old roundup cook who happened by if there was anything I could do to make it more palatable. He said: "Why, yes, sure ma'am, just fill your milk pans half full of cold water and then fill them up with milk."

I was almost sure he was joking—but nevertheless I tried it, only to find, of course, that the milk tasted just as much of onion as ever. Perhaps he answered me that way just to be funny, and thinking that anybody would know better. But if he *was* making fun of my ignorance, then he was the first mean man I'd met in Montana!

Parties were held every so often in our countryside, by anybody who had a room big enough—and it didn't have to be very big. They would hold them in winter when the work was light, and people would drive to them from miles and miles away, all bundled up in a wagon with their babies in their arms. They would sprinkle corn meal on the rough floors to make them slippery, and the men tramping in and out would track in snow which would mix with the corn meal to make a kind of slush, so your skirt would be wet way above the hem, but nobody stopped dancing for that. The few women present would be danced half to death. And it lasted till morning, because you couldn't drive home anyway until it was daylight.

I didn't go to many of these parties after my babies came. I remember one time when a road ranch only ten miles out of Miles City was holding a big public dance, for money, of course, they sent a messenger clear up into our country, nearly a hundred miles, to ask people to come. I told the boy I couldn't go, on account of the baby.

"Oh, but Maw has a room where she puts the babies," he said.

This was unusual elegance. At most of the dances the babies were simply laid on the floor under the benches where the spectators sat. Apparently most women were more willing to pack their small children around the country than I was; but I just couldn't.

The spring of '85 seventeen-year-old Fanny Young, who had been a neighbor when we lived over on Lame Deer, came with a friend of hers to visit us.

Of course that was reason enough for all the bachelors far and near to visit us, and it doubled my work.
But youth isn't always thoughtful, and it never occurred to the girls that I might need help. They
would sit down after breakfast and play pitch with
the rest of them to see who would wash the dishes
—but they never once offered to lend a hand with
the cooking—what they liked was to go out and
ride with the men. Mr. Alderson was so annoyed he
wanted to drop them a few hints on the subject of
helping, but I wouldn't let him.

When I said that the boys came to see the two girls,
I should have said that they came principally to see
Miss Young. Her friend, Miss S. I will call her, was
a very bright young woman but very advanced for
our day. She scandalized our boys, who were rather
old-fashioned, by borrowing their trousers and riding
astride; when the rest of us, if we did have to ride a
man's saddle, would simply crook a knee over the
saddle horn. Miss S. was very energetic, too, and
always wanted to work with them, hauling poles or
helping stretch wire. They admired her intellect,
but they were rather nonplussed.

Some time later this same young woman married
a most conservative man, older than she, and the
last man in the world I should have expected. My
husband and I dined with them one time in Miles
City, and I wore out Mr. Alderson's shins kicking

them under the table, I was so afraid he would mention the trousers.

Still later, a matter of years, I met her again. She had been living some time on a ranch with her husband, and in the course of our conversation she told me of some girls from Miles City who had been out to visit her. She complained that they were so thoughtless, they were interested in nothing except riding around with the men, never offering to help her, nor seeming to realize the extra work that they caused!

I thought then: How circumstances can change a point of view!

In its small way the two girls' visit was a turning point for me. It was not until then that I began to grow up—always a painful process. Only a year before, *I* had been the one who went riding—and I loved to ride; I had been the center of attention; I had been free to have a good time. Now it was others who had the fun, while I had only the hard work. And I didn't like it one bit. It would have helped, if just once one of them had said: "Now I'll stay and get dinner and mind the baby today, and you go for a ride." But none of them ever did say it. And I began to feel that I was really very greatly abused.

To add to my feelings of injury, I was left alone all night for the first time since coming to Montana —or since I was born. At the end of Miss Young's visit she and Miss S. invited all the boys to go back with them for a party. Oh, they invited me too, of course, but I couldn't go—there was the baby, and then, too, Mr. Alderson was away and I thought I shouldn't leave. A strange boy had come in to see about getting a job; he was planning to wait for Mr. Alderson, and I urged Brown, who had been left in charge, to go along with the rest of them, since the boy could stay with me till he returned. They all said they were coming back the following night.

What followed was simply due to a misunderstanding. For twenty-four hours the strange boy stayed on the premises. The next afternoon, after filling the wood box and bringing in the water, he asked me if I was afraid of being alone just a little while, as he wanted to ride down the river and see about another job. I said "Of course not"—because I expected Brown back, and the rest of them.

But Brown didn't come back, because he thought the strange boy was with me, and I passed a scared and miserable night alone with the baby. I remember one of my preparations for the siege was to go out and collar Mr. Zook's dog and bring him inside, because I was afraid he'd bark at a coyote, and scare me to death.

The next afternoon, just when I was beginning to dread the prospect of another night alone, they all came trooping in, full of high spirits. I was so relieved, I cried. Then they all felt terribly, which soothed my feelings and made me feel ashamed of myself. So I begged them to stay, and told them I'd make them some waffles for supper. We were in the middle of the waffles, when Mr. Alderson came home.

I talked as fast as I could, but it was no use. Brown blurted out the truth. And in all the years we were married, I never saw Mr. Alderson so angry. He was going to fire Brown, and I pleaded with him all evening and way into the night before I persuaded him to change his mind.

The experience taught me something I never forgot. I saw that I was beginning to feel sorry for myself—the lowest state to which a woman's mind can fall. And I made up my mind to stop it. Many times in the years that followed I forgot this worthy resolve, but I always came back to it sooner or later. I still think it the most important lesson that any wife can learn, whether she lives in a house of cottonwood logs or in a palace.

Chapter XI

WHILE WE WERE ON TONGUE RIVER THE CHEY-
ennes were all around us, the same Indians with
whom we had twice had trouble through no fault
of our own. One of our neighbors was Black Wolf,
whom Hal shot and whose lodge burned our home.
One winter morning a few months after my arrival,
just as we were finishing breakfast, Black Wolf came
in. He announced that he had a sick papoose, and

wanted milk. Mr. Alderson invited him to sit down and have some coffee while I was straining the milk into the bottle. There was a piece of steak on the platter in front of him, and when I set his coffee down he pointed first to the steak and then to the stove, as a sign that he wished me to cook it some more. This made me so mad—when I knew the old heathen often ate meat raw, with the blood running down his chin—that I told him I wasn't going to cook it for him; he could eat it the way it was or go without. Although he didn't understand English he appeared to catch the drift, for he concluded to eat the steak "as is."

It was two braves of Black Wolf's lodge who admitted at the trial that they were the ones who set fire to our home, and were sent to the penitentiary. One of them died in prison, and the Indian Bureau later circulated a petition to have the other one pardoned, with the result that he was given his freedom. As soon as he reached home, he walked ten miles to spend the day with us! We wouldn't have known him from any other Indian, but he made us understand, with the sign language and a few English words, that he had burned our "tepee." He further informed us, with gestures, that he had had his hands tied together and had gone for a long ride on a train ("Choo-choo-choo"); that his comrade had "gone to sleep"; that he himself had now come home to stay. He seemed to believe we would be glad to see him!

Other Indians told us that one of the bucks who set fire to our house was one of the two whom we took in and fed and sheltered that stormy night. Somehow words fail me at this point. Our relations with our Indian neighbors were, to say the least, perplexing.

I persuaded one of them, a squaw named Rattlesnake, to come (when the spirit moved her) and do our washing, while her daughter, a comely, tidy looking (for an Indian) sixteen-year-old girl looked after the baby. I had quite a time over this girl's name. Whenever I asked it she would look sullen, and she and the mother would jabber away at each other, without answering me. One day the interpreter from the agency came over with them, so I asked him to find out what the young squaw's name was. He talked with them a minute and then said: "She doesn't want you to know her name. She doesn't like it."

I said: "Tell her we white folks often don't like our names either, and if she will tell me hers I will give her a pretty one."

Her name was Bob-Tailed Horse. No wonder the child objected! I told the interpreter to tell her I would call her Minnehaha. She and her mother tried out the first part of this name, repeating it several times with a pleased expression. "Mee-nee!" So that was settled.

Minnie made a good and faithful nurse, when she chose to come, carrying the baby on her back as she was carried when she was a papoose, and crooning songs to her. Indians are unquestionably fond of children. They will snatch them out of mischief, give them a little shake and grunt at them, and there it ends. After that the child is simply removed from temptation, and I have never seen one of them spank a small child.

Our baby started walking at fourteen months, but her little shoes were so slick on the soles, from the polishing they got on the dry grass, that she fell until she grew discouraged. So I asked Minnie to make her a pair of moccasins. A few days later she brought a prettily beaded pair and put them on the baby, who was so delighted to find she could walk without falling, that she walked a hundred miles, I'm sure, the first day.

It was all very kindly up to a point, but beyond the kindness there was a blank wall. In view of the cruelties that had been exchanged between white man and Indian, it was no wonder if real warmth was lacking between them, or if the Indian attitude toward us was one of complete cynicism. I can understand this now, but at the time I was terribly disappointed. I came from the South, and despite the burning of our house I looked, unconsciously perhaps, for the same affectionate relationship with the Indians that had existed in my old home between the colored people and the whites. One of the hard lessons I had to learn in Montana was that the affection I sentimentally wanted just simply was not there —with one deeply touching exception which happened later.

But genuinely friendly or not, they were with us, and with white neighbors as few and far between as ever, they were our principal diversion. Following on the heels of Minnie and Rattlesnake came all their kin. Sometimes we would have seven or eight to feed—the extra ones arriving at meal time. We learned to look forward to their visits as a certainty on rainy days—I don't know why, unless it was because their tepees were smoky when the atmosphere was heavy, and the white man's fire was warmer.

One of our steady visitors was an old woman we called Granny. I think she was some kind of a relative of Iron Shirt, the man whom Packsaddle Jack shot in the arm. As soon as it rained, here would come Granny to sit by the fire, bringing in with her a fine, ripe smell of grease and unwashed Indian, and a great many muddy tracks. Particularly impressive was the broad, muddy imprint which she left where she sat. Once I scolded her for tracking up my floor and told her she couldn't come again, but when she showed up next time with a gunny sack to wrap her feet in, I didn't have the heart to send her back to her tepee. Always she sat and sat, stolid and unmoving, rarely saying anything even though she stayed all day. But one day when she was there the baby was naughty, and as my patience was exhausted from many repetitions, I picked her up and spanked her.

At that the old squaw flew at me in a rage, yelling I don't know what insults in loudest Cheyenne, and jerking the baby from me. Perhaps she was right on the spanking issue and I was wrong, but at the moment I was in no mood to be set right by a Cheyenne squaw as to how I should bring up my child. So I snatched the baby back, and then I took Granny by the shoulders and shoved her outdoors, telling her that she was "hyper-siba" (no good), and that she could go to her tepee and not sit by my fire any more.

When my husband came in and I told him about it he laughed, but then he grew serious. He told me that I had done a very dangerous thing, for the squaws often fought each other, sometimes with knives. I remembered then that they always carried sharp butcher knives in their belts, and that not so long before one had come to see me with a deep cut on her arm, which she informed me a "hyper-siba" squaw had given her.

However, in two days Granny was back. She appeared at the window, showed me her gunny sack for wrapping up her muddy feet, and we buried the hatchet. Insofar as there was any communion of feeling between our strange neighbors and ourselves it existed through the baby. One fall while we were on Tongue River a band of Piegans came from the north of us to run off some Cheyenne horses. I don't remember whether or not the raid was successful, but at any rate one of the Piegans was killed and scalped. The scalp lock was then stretched over a willow branch, and the gruesome object was sent from one Cheyenne camp to another, where it was an occasion of feasting and dancing. We had heard the tom-toms for several nights, and we knew we could not expect to see Minnie or Rattlesnake for several days. So we decided to take coffee, sugar and beef and attend the dance.

On this night it was a dance of the young squaws, and was held in a big tepee lighted by a central fire. The Indian men were seated about one edge of the tepee, the squaws on the other side. My husband and our cowboys took seats with the men, the baby and I among the squaws. The ceremonial pipe was passed to the men, all taking a puff and passing it back to the chief, while the scalp lock was passed from hand to hand. Then the tom-toms started and two young squaws got up, facing away from the fire. They danced holding their knees stiff and moving from side to side with short hops. One of the squaws would touch one of the young men with the toe of her moccasin and he would take his place between the two, facing the fire. Then they would all dance around the circle; then two more squaws would replace the dancers, the young man going back to his side of the tepee and the squaws to theirs. The young men wore white sheets about their heads and shoulders, only their eyes showing, but when they were chosen to dance, they let fall the sheet and stood up clothed in moccasins, leggings, bear claw necklace and loin cloth, sometimes with the body painted as well as the face.

After all this had been going on awhile, Minnie came and got our baby, with many grunts and smiles, placing her between herself and another squaw, facing the fire. Mabel was a beautiful little girl, with big blue eyes and golden curls, and as she stood up there between the two squaws with the firelight on her happy face, she made a picture that none of us ever forgot. Minnie had taught her the squaw dance, and now she didn't hesitate a minute, but kept perfect time and step. Even the stolid old Indians smiled and grunted their approval. "Good papoose, good papoose," they kept saying, as she went around with Minnie and said goodbye to every Indian in the tepee. That she felt no fear seemed to please them immensely.

Yes, it was a strange relationship. Not very long before or after the dance, I remember something else happening which shows the other side of the white man-Indian contact. The fact that this second incident occured very largely inside my own head does not alter its significance. My husband and I were kindly people, I believe; yet the truce with our red neighbors was never anything but a truce until their threat was utterly broken.

This rather foolish little thing happened on a wash day. Rattlesnake failed me, so I had to do the work myself. A man who was living with us temporarily, and who was the only one home at the time, carried the water for my washtubs before he left for the day. Mr. Alderson, Johnny Zook and our two regular boys were away on the roundup, and Mr. Alderson had arranged with this man to stay and look after me. He had some horses out on the range and today he left as usual to ride after them, saying he would only be gone an hour or so.

Noon came, two o'clock, then three o'clock and no man. I put the baby to bed for her afternoon nap, sat down and started imagining things. Quite a number of Sioux had passed by there that morning on a visit, and I got to thinking that they might be planning an outbreak. *There is nothing a woman left alone on a ranch can't imagine when she is afraid.* I carried more water to finish the washing. Then I brought in a lot of wood, thinking I'd have to keep up the fire all night; by this time I was sure the man wasn't coming back, and I knew that if I were by myself I couldn't sleep. Next I decided to give the cow some hay, and I took the baby down in the carriage and left her outside the corral while I pulled the hay down with my hands.

On this trip or one of the many I made into the yard to see if my protector was coming, I saw what seemed to be Indians on the bluff across the river, ducking from tree to tree, first in plain sight, then disappearing. By this time I was thinking of all the horrors I had ever heard about what Indians had done to babies and women; picking babies up and knocking them against trees; scalping women and shooting them full of arrows and worse. I fled into the house, picked the baby up, and holding her in my arms, knelt down beside the window and prayed.

Next time I looked across the river I saw three squaws sitting on the river bank, taking off their moccasins preparing to wade across. They were Indians I knew, and they were bringing some berries for sale! I had even been expecting them. Their appearing and disappearing on the opposite river bank was simply because of the crooked path that wound among the trees.

I was so glad to see them that I overpaid them recklessly for the berries. But enough of the fright remained so I gave them a note to carry to our nearest neighbor, two and a half miles up the river, asking him to come and stay with me.

Soon after he arrived the other man came back. He had been all day hunting horses, having been the victim of a mild Indian scare of his own. He too had seen the Sioux and, believing they had run his horses off, had followed them for miles down the river, only to find on returning that the horses were just where he had expected to find them.

Chapter XII

FROM THE FALL OF 1884, WHEN I LEFT MILES CITY
with the baby, to the spring of 1886, when I took
her home for a visit to my mother and grandmother,
I never saw Miles City or civilization, and indeed I
hardly ever left the ranch. I don't remember that the
baby and I were off it at all during one entire summer. This was not as bad as it sounds. It's true that
the things of art and society were lacking; human
nature supplied all the interest we had; but there

was plenty of human nature in a ranch country, and plenty of opportunity to ponder its odd quirks. While we had few neighbors, we knew those few with a day-by-day intimacy that city people today never approach. I fear there was hardly any such thing as one's private affairs—but the lack of privacy was made up for by the tolerance, the rich affection and understanding which the neighbors in our sparsely settled country had for one another.

When we moved onto Tongue River George Brewster, a former Yankee, was ranching a few miles up the river from us. Before we left Captain Brown of Mississippi had moved in very near, with his young southern wife, and the wife's cousin, Miss Mary Peachey Roberts, had come to visit them. So if we had stayed on Tongue River I should have had two lovely lady neighbors only two and a half miles away. But instead I promptly moved out into another wilderness—which was why people said I couldn't stand civilization.

Year after year the fiery little Confederate veteran and the Massachusetts Republican ran their cattle on the divides back of Tongue River; year after year they went on the roundup together, good neighbors and friends—until election year came around, when they would fight out their differences in deadly battle every night in the big tent, before a gallery of discreetly amused cowboys. And when the election was over they would bury the hatchet and go on as before. There was always a great deal of moving around in the West; and a great deal of giving up and going back East when things grew hard. But the community on Tongue River held together and grew. My husband's younger brother, Lew Alderson, married Miss Roberts' younger sister and joined it; nearly everybody who came was a relative of somebody else who had come before, and today there are half a score of hard-riding ranch families living within a few miles of each other, whose friendship is in its third generation, with a fourth generation coming up. I mention this to show that the whole truth about the so-called wild West has not been told in the movies.

Although we loved our neighbors in the old days —on the whole and after making due allowances— that fact didn't keep us from enjoying their foibles. While living on Tongue River I saw living disproof of the old belief that while no house was big enough for two women, any house was big enough for two men. There were a number of bachelor households around us, within hailing distance, so to speak. It was a common arrangement out here for the young man who didn't have money to take in a partner who did, and the two of them would live together and divide the work. I noticed that they fell out just about as often as two women would have done, and for reasons that weren't any better. Each one would think he was doing more than his share, or they would get on each other's nerves in the long winter months, and would disagree over little things just the way women do.

My household on Tongue River varied in size according to the season, but we always had extras, and some of them would be permanent over quite a long period. One of the semi-permanents was Packsaddle Jack. After the trouble with Iron Shirt blew over, he came back and spent the winter with us as before. And that was the time he froze his face and nearly got gangrene, just because he was too stubborn to do anything anyone suggested.

Mr. Alderson was sending a small issue of beef to the Indians, and Packsaddle and Brown were taking them over the divide. It was bitterly cold, and since there is nothing so deadly in cold weather as riding at a slow pace behind cattle, Mr. Alderson had cautioned them both to get off and walk. Packsaddle, of course, wouldn't do it. Brown, walking along in front and leading his horse, looked back—to find that Packsaddle, as he said later, "couldn't have been any whiter if he was dead." Although his nose and cheeks and ears were quite stiff, he refused even then to get off and let Brown rub him with snow, grumbling that when they got over to Lame Deer he'd get some coal oil and rub his face with that. (All cowboys had a

fixed belief that with coal oil they could cure anything.)

But when they got over the top of the divide a
warm wind struck him and thawed him out too fast,
with appalling results. They hurried home to us
next day, to be there for Christmas, and I never have
seen such a sight. His face was green and blue and
purple, while as for his ears, I never thought a
human ear could swell to such a size or stick out so
far. Such a terrible crack appeared between his ear
and his head, that I thought his ear must come off;
I dropped warm glycerine on it with a turkey feather,
and that was all we could do in the way of first aid.
Luck was with us on that occasion as it was on so
many others. We lived so far from a doctor, that
time and again it was only our guardian angel and
our good constitutions that saved us.

With settlers coming into the country so fast there
was a good deal of travel up and down Tongue River,
and a week never passed that we didn't have visitors.
They came and stayed exactly as they pleased; we
obeyed the law of western hospitality and took in
all comers, whoever they might be. There were plenty
of road ranches by this time, where people took
transients and charged them for bed and board, but
road ranches were something different. None of the
stockmen ever charged; that was their custom and
their pride.

One evening when Mr. Alderson was home from the roundup for the night, three men rode in. There was nothing remarkable about them to my eye, except that one of their number was a fair young boy who quite won my heart, he looked so young and well-raised. After supper they all played pitch for the dish-washing, and two of the strangers did it. When we were alone, Mr. Alderson said: "I don't like their looks." They had been evasive about their business, but had taken an interest in the gun rack in the hallway.

I said: "Oh, but that's such a nice young boy who is with them."

"Yes," Mr. Alderson replied, "I guess he's just gotten in bad company." He thought they were there to steal horses from the Cheyennes. I said: "How can you be so sure?" Next morning they left, with no further incident except that they bought a gun from Alec Brown, a Kansas boy who was building fences for us that year.

A few weeks later we saw in the paper that two men were caught stealing horses somewhere near the North Dakota line; that there had been a fight, and a young boy with them had been killed. The descriptions tallied, and we felt sure they were our visitors.

One night, I think it was later that same season, a half-breed Indian stopped with us. The bunk room was furnished with plain iron bedsteads on which the boys' roundup beds were spread out, and one of these we reserved for "doubtful" visitors—as distinct from friends or cowboys. We gave this bed to the Indian, and next morning he went on his way, leaving lice behind him. But we never knew anything about it until some weeks later, when it got so cold that Brown and Packsaddle raided the doubtful bed for extra blankets, without telling me anything about it. In no time they were overrun.

The next few weeks were the worst nightmare I have ever experienced. We boiled those blankets in water with lye in it, but could do only two at a time, for it was bitterly cold, and the boys couldn't be left without covers. Mr. Alderson and I would crunch out over the snow to the clothesline, I in my clumsy fleece-lined overshoes and Mr. Zook's buffalo coat, carrying the wash boiler between us. And we would lift the blankets out of the boiling water with a stick and they would freeze stiff almost before we got the clothespins in them. They had to freeze dry; I can't explain the process except to say that they hung on the line and froze and froze, and when we took them down they were soft. But it took four or five days.

Meanwhile we kept the boys busy applying remedies. What made it so unbearably difficult was keeping the infected blankets from contaminating the clean ones, with the weather so cold and only just so many covers to go around. We finally managed it by cleaning up one bed at a time, and one boy. But the boiling and freezing and scrubbing lasted for weeks, and was such a horror that I woke up every morning to a feeling of dread.

Shortly after the end of this siege four men rode in one evening across the frozen hills. They were the sheriff of Custer County, his deputy, the biggest stockman in our part of Montana—and a prisoner. I knew the last—a harmless fellow we had always thought him, who lived among the Indians, with no real job. They called him Cheyenne Charlie. He was some kind of a foreigner, I don't know what, but I know he was troubled by his poor English, for he had told me that he had sisters and that he was the only member of his family who "talked broken." He had been to our house before, and I had given him an old homemade fur-trimmed cap to keep his ears warm. I think he was accused of butchering the big cattleman's beef.

Perhaps because of our previous acquaintance, the poor fellow was so embarrassed at the removal of handcuffs while he ate, that I could hardly keep the tears from falling into his coffee while I poured it. One of the men said later that no one could have told from the treatment they received which was the cattle king and which the man under arrest. I thought this one of the nicest compliments I had ever had.

Next morning they were all with us for breakfast. There were not enough cups to go round, with the extras at table, so I used jelly glasses and tin cups, cautioning Mr. Alderson to see to it that the guests got the good cups and saucers, but of course it came out the other way. The officers talked, while the poor prisoner ate in silence. Custer County had not been subdivided then but was a territory as large as many eastern states, and the sheriff was a power in the county. He was a seasoned-looking man, heavily built, with the long mustaches which all the men wore in that day, and keen, piercing eyes. His deputy appeared more citified or eastern; I know he worked for one of the large ranches; it may have been as bookkeeper. But both were alike in gentlemanliness. Wherever he came from, the deputy gave me the impression of being enthusiastic about the west. He had a young, vivacious wife living in Miles City, and he complimented me on the gingham apron I was wearing, and asked me for the pattern, so he could give it to her. He said he did like to see a housewife wearing an apron. When I came to Miles City, he added, I must be sure to meet his wife and let her entertain me.

The sheriff was equally kind, though in a connection I found less enjoyable. Mr. Alderson insisted upon entertaining the visitors with an account of our ordeal with the lice! I was embarrassed, but he treated it as a joke. When he had finished the sheriff turned to me and said: "Mrs. Alderson, we've been riding all over the country and stopping everywhere, and there is no telling what we've picked up. We may leave them with you again. I want you to promise me that if we do, you'll send Custer County a good, big bill!"

I did go to Miles City a few months later, on my way home to West Virginia. And his wife did call on me and invite me to her apartment—an "apartment" in Miles City then being rooms over a store— to meet a number of other ladies. She was so dainty and pretty—a perfect little watch charm of a woman —and so beautifully dressed. If she had ever found use for the apron pattern it was not in evidence. I remember well the California cordial which she served, because I do not usually like anything alcoholic but I liked that. And I remember the sparkling little cut-glass cordial glasses in which she served it. I couldn't help contrasting all this with the tin cup we had offered her husband at our house, and that was one of the moments when I gave way to feeling sorry for myself. But when I mentioned the tin cup she said, "Oh, but he had *such* a good time!"

Chapter XIII

SPRING HAD COME TO MONTANA WHEN I TOOK THE
baby and went home for a long visit to my mother
and grandmother. But first I stopped in Miles City
to buy clothes suitable for the journey, and there
our two-year-old ranch baby had her first glimpse
of civilization. One day, in the lobby of the Mac-
Queen House, she met a little girl; I knew the mother
slightly, and as we chatted the little ones scraped

acquaintance. I don't know how it happened—but in a minute Mabel had slapped the first white child she ever saw.

For the rest, she was friendly with everybody. On the train she called the porter and the waiters in the dining car "Cheyennes," much to their amusement. On the ranch, the only prettily dressed women she saw were the colored prints in the Altman and Stern catalogues, and she always called them "pretty mamas." I stopped with an old friend in St. Paul to do some more shopping, and when we went into a big store, Mabel would rush up to the young lady clerks, calling them pretty mamas. My friend would explain that the child had always lived on a ranch in Montana and seen few people except Indians; that she was now going to visit her grandmother and great-grandmother in Virginia. This invariably produced a sensation; the whole store would gather round, and Mabel, encouraged by my friend, would chatter Cheyenne. Although it is one of the most difficult languages known, she could talk it better than she could English—Minnie having proved an effective teacher.

The child's beauty and unusual ways drew people to her. My mother was impressed by her charm, and enjoyed taking Mabel to see her friends—exhibiting her, as it were. The little girl had an Indian doll which Minnie had shaped, with amazing skill, out of buckskin—a perfect image of a Cheyenne squaw. Its hair was of buffalo mane, carefully braided. It had leggings, and prettily beaded moccasins, and a gay colored shawl. Minnie had taught her to carry it on her back like a papoose. But after a few days in Virginia the contrary young lady discarded her Indian doll and started demanding a doll such as other white children had, and she would no longer speak a word of Cheyenne.

I, of course, boasted of my household accomplishments, and in telling how I had learned to make good biscuits I mentioned the long-necked wine bottle that I used to roll out my dough—a trick I had learned from the men. At that grandmother gave me a startled look.

"What a Godforsaken country you chose to live in, Nannie!" she exclaimed, and at once went to a store and bought me a rolling pin.

I enjoyed settling down to a life of being waited on; I enjoyed the leisure, but what struck me first and hardest was the flowers. Even before we reached St. Paul I was catching my breath over them as I looked out the train window; after three years of no flowers but wild ones, even a geranium on a window sill seemed a flame of loveliness. The green lawns affected me in the same way after our sun-baked, barren-seeming country, and so did the trees and their deep, peaceful shade. Indoors I was conscious of two things—the high ceilings, so spacious after a low, log roof—and the closets.

But if I had any regrets, even mild ones, I don't remember them now. I had had all the comforts and many luxuries in my growing years; they had never given me great happiness, and I had lost all feeling of dependence on them. I never learned it again, not even for the little things, for what people call conveniences. I could always get along without them. The small things of civilization are very nice, but I'm sorry for people who fuss too much over them.

Our second little girl was born in West Virginia in August, and we called her Fay Sue. I didn't go back to Montana till the following March, and in that way I missed the hard winter, the worst in the history of the West. But I found nothing the same afterwards. From then onwards, even the illusion of prosperity vanished.

There had been signs even before the hard winter that the cattle business was not all we thought it. In '84 or '85 there was a stockyards strike in Chicago and the cattle couldn't be shipped; after Mr. Zook and Mr. Alderson had gathered all their steers and brought them into Miles City they had to take them all the way home again and turn them back out on the range. So there were no profits from the sale of beef steers that year; and the next year prices began to slip.

A short while before this we had received fabulous offers for the business—that is, simply for the cattle, buildings and range rights, since no one owned any land. In the light of after events Mr. Zook and Mr. Alderson may have been foolish to refuse, but what else could they do? I remember when were at Lame Deer an easterner came to the ranch and wanted to buy. He had a foreman with him and he was looking over the country and buying cattle. Mr. Alderson said to him: "If we sold to you we'd have to turn right around and locate all over again"—and with prices what they were then he would have been bound to lose.

Then too we had hard luck in our first year, and heavy expenses with our first two children. When I went to Miles City and the first baby was born, our house was burned, and I had to stay and board for seven months. Meanwhile there was all the expense of moving the outfit and building the new house; a log house cost a lot to build even in those days, even though our second one was of inferior cottonwood logs instead of pine. The firm had to borrow money to pay for all this. Part of the time they were paying eighteen percent for it. Finally, because I'd had such a miserable time in Miles City before, I went home to West Virginia for my second baby. We would never have decided on that expense if we had known what hard times were ahead.

Mr. Alderson came east to join me after Thanksgiving, but when reports of the winter began reaching him he became horribly worried and anxious to get back. We started home in March, as soon as he felt we could get through to the ranch. As it was, we were the first to try to break trail. Coming through North Dakota, the snow was so deep that we had to have a snow plow and two engines most of the time, and often the only way we knew the train had stopped at a town was by seeing the tops of houses above the great drifts. When we reached Miles City everyone told us we could never make it. But my husband knew that if we hoped to get to the ranch we must start now or be indefinitely delayed, for the bright sun was already softening the ice in the rivers, and threatening to unleash the spring floods, and we had countless river and creek crossings to make.

We started out comfortably with a pair of strong horses hitched to a bobsled, our baggage and a newly employed man stowed in the back, while my husband, myself and the two children occupied the front seat of the sleigh. Our first overnight stop was Piper Dan's, the same road ranch where I had had my first ranch dinner as a bride. I'm sure that just as I was the first bride to take dinner at Piper Dan's, I was also the first mother with two babies to stop with him. He did his best to cope with the emergency, but I couldn't help contrasting this visit with the one I had made four years earlier. I was a girl then, and every little hardship was a game, but now it was all grimly serious. Fortunately, babies, when tired, are not very discriminating.

Notwithstanding conditions we must have slept well, for when we arose the next morning, thinking to make an early start, we found it was snowing. And we were traveling in an open box sled! My husband with his usual resource, however, went to the river bank, and with the help of our new hand, John Logan, cut a number of willow poles. These he bent into half hoops which he fastened at intervals along the box body of our sled, thus duplicating, in effect, the top frame of a covered wagon. Now it only required to cover these with a wagon sheet, and our bobsled was completely enclosed and sheltered from the worst the weather man could send. The body of the sled was then filled with sweet blue grass hay and after that a number of buffalo robes and blankets were included for warmth. I must say, it looked inviting enough for a one-day's journey, but I was to travel five days in these narrow quarters with the two babies. The hundred miles to the ranch were often covered, with a good team, in two days under fair conditions, but just now innumerable snowdrifts lay across our path. We were digging out of the drifts all the time. One day we traveled from sunup to sundown and only made ten miles.

For four days the children and I were cramped down there in the bottom of the sled along with the baggage, unable to see out. I am sure that every dent and scar on those old trunks is indelibly imprinted on my mind. There was no place to make a baby comfortable, so I just held her in my arms; she was seven months old, and it was just as tiring for her as it was for me. The fact that the children's ages differed—one being an infant and the other a restless three-year-old—made my task no easier, and I told stories and sang Mother Goose rhymes to Mabel until I felt idiotic. In between I whiled away the time for myself by thinking longingly of all the good things I'd had to eat at Mother's. Every so often I would lift up the side to see out or let Mabel see out, until forced to close it down again on account of the cold.

On the road we met the first team to come down the river that spring—for they hadn't been able to get out because of the snow. After we passed them we tried to follow their track, but the new snow that fell filled it in. It was a depressing trip; Miles City had been full of talk about the dreadful losses, and we passed by several places where the cattle were piled up in frozen heaps. I remember one place in particular where the road followed around under a bank, with rocks and a small shelf up above. They had squeezed in under the rocks for shelter until no more could squeeze in, and had died.

There were quite a few road ranches on the river road by this time, and the stages were easy, but there had been no teams to Miles City for supplies, and all the cupboards were bare. We had only salt pork for meat, as the starving cattle were too thin for beef, and the only tea we had was at Mr. Liscom's. The rest of the time I had to drink coffee, which was bad for the baby; it was sweetened with molasses, since the sugar had run out, and the dried apples were sweetened the same way. Prices were terribly high; Mr. Alderson said it cost us as much to get to the ranch as it did to come on the Pullman to Miles City. There had been no travel, and we were the first victims.

However, two pleasant things happened on the way. The first was the stop at George Liscom's excellent ranch; the next was disguised as an accident. When we were trying to make a river crossing our sled runners cut through the upper ice and there we were, stalled; but luckily we had picked a spot across from a comfortable-looking house. When the family discovered our plight the men came down to the bank, and finding a woman and two children they insisted that we come in while the sled was pulled out. The top of the ice was all wet and sloppy from a thaw, so they carried us across. Inside we found two lovely ladies. One was the woman of the house; the other was the school teacher whom she had engaged for her children. This school teacher turned into a lifelong friend—and before many years she was our partner's wife.

Next morning we went on, to more days of floundering through drifts, of struggling with the honeycombed ice which caved in under us at the edge of the river crossings. Just two and a half miles below our ranch we came to the Browns. During my stay in West Virginia Captain Brown had brought his wife and Cousin Peachey to Tongue River, and we stopped to say "howdy" to them. Although their first experience of a Montana winter—snowed in as they were from fall to spring—must have been anything but encouraging to young ladies from Mississippi, they seemed most cheerful. The babies and I were too bundled up to get out of the sleigh, so we just visited for a few minutes. In a little while longer we were home.

My husband began riding the range at once—and now we found something to encourage us. For we had not lost as heavily as most of our neighbors. My husband had weaned his calves the previous November, thus giving the cows a chance to get stronger before the snow got so deep. He was the first man to wean in our part of Montana; not only that, but he winter-fed too. He had a lot of good grass on the divide at the head of Muddy. He had stacked this and built corrals up there in the fall, and when the snow covered all the feed Mr. Zook and Brown rode out when they could, and gathered up what cattle they could find and fed them. This saved many of our cattle—more than most people saved—but we lost heavily nevertheless.

Chapter XIV

WE STAYED ONLY A FEW MORE MONTHS ON TONGUE River, as my husband and Mr. Zook had decided to break their partnership. Five years had been the term of the original agreement, and the five years were up. It was a good time to dissolve, because the cattle had to be tallied that spring to see what was left after the hard winter. But Mr. Alderson and I had never expected to give up our home.

163

It happened this way. In dividing the assets, the two partners would take turn about at setting a value on this or that item; when one had priced it, the other must take it or leave it at that figure. The ranch, the house and the furniture were all lumped together; Mr. Zook had the pricing of them, and he named a figure which Mr. Alderson felt was too high. Thus it came about that Mr. Zook kept the house and everything in it. Mr. Alderson took his interest in cattle. He located a new ranch near the head of Muddy Creek on the Rosebud, ten miles from our first home. And we moved for the third time in four years.

Mr. Alderson had just time enough to make a trip to Miles City before the roundup started, and come back with one wagon load of bare necessities. He brought a cook stove, some provisions, and a few chairs. He also brought two mirrors. That was absolutely all we had to start with.

Some little time before this the government had started an agency for the Cheyennes, on the site of our old ranch on Lame Deer. The first agent's wife, Mrs. Upshaw, had stayed with us in the spring of 1885, while their house was being built. She now repaid us in kind, by inviting me and the children to stay with her. One day in May she sent an Indian over with a wagon to get us. I loaded the children in, with our clothes and some personal pictures, and that was our moving day. We stayed with Mrs. Upshaw for perhaps two weeks, but as soon as the new house had a roof and a floor we moved into it, even before the clay daubing between the logs was finished. And that was when I began to pioneer in earnest. In many ways this was going back to the beginning—or worse than the beginning, since we were no longer borne up by the belief that our trials were temporary. Once more we were living in two rooms, with a tent outside for the boys to live in during the summer. (When winter came we built two bunks in the kitchen.) We had board floors, but they were put down rough and unplaned. Fay was crawling, and there was the problem of splinters—so I cut a sugar sack in two and hung it over her shoulders with suspenders, thus keeping her clean, besides saving her knees. One of our neighbor stockmen came to see us one day, and was quite taken by Fay's costume.

"Wait till she gets to be sixteen," he said. "Then I'll tell her I knew her when she wore gunny sack dresses."

That fall when Jack, the motherless calf, was sold as a five-year-old steer, I bought a carpet for the bedroom. And as soon as I could I diamond-dyed the kitchen floor brown and oiled it so it wouldn't show grease spots. For furniture, I improvised a couch out of two Arbuckle coffee cases and some boards, padding the top with what the boys called a "sougan," and I called a comfort—the latter taken out of an old roundup bed. Our new hand, Mr. Logan, was very handy with tools, and he made us bedsteads and a bureau. The latter had no drawers, but it had shelves which I covered with cretonne. We made out very well, for make out we must. But I can truthfully say that the six years spent on Muddy were the hardest of my life.

Years later when I was a widow living on another ranch, I had a near neighbor and friend who had moved to the West for reasons of health. She told me that when she was packing to come she debated a long time whether to take her few pieces of silver, her books, her pictures—they seemed so inappropriate to the hard, simple life she was planning to lead. She decided finally in their favor, and she never ceased to be thankful, for those few little luxuries which she had hesitated to bring were all that saved her.

"At times they were all that helped me to keep my head up," she said. "I'd have died without them."

I know just what she meant—for after the fire I had nothing of that sort to cling to.

On Muddy I was more alone than I had ever been. Mr. Alderson was away as much as ever, and we had less help because we had cut down the number of our cattle. So I had less of the boys' cheery companionship, and we were so remote that visitors were few. Tongue River was a thoroughfare, but no white people except ourselves had business up this narrow, lonely valley. Above us our horses ran on the high, windswept divide; below us the valley wound downhill for ten miles before getting anywhere—and "anywhere," when reached, was nothing but a tiny log postoffice, a few houses, and Mr. Young's store.

But the worst of hardships was the consciousness of getting run down at the heel. You *had* to keep up or go under—and keeping up made much hard work. I'm a vain old woman now and I was vain then, and I struggled for daintiness. Yet I never liked to ask for anything because Mr. Alderson was so hard up for cash. Not that we didn't have credit—we had too much credit!

My own clothes gave me no trouble. The good ones that I brought with me or bought in Miles City lasted for years, and when they gave out I made myself gingham dresses of pretty colors. Once or twice I even had a nice Alsatian girl to help with the sewing.

I made all the children's clothes, of course. For several years I dressed Fay and Mabel in a sort of a uniform, a blue and white gingham apron with a sash and a turned-down collar. Children's play overalls had not yet been invented, and it took eight apiece of these pinafores to keep them clean, one for each day of the week and the eighth to carry them over. Even though we did live out in the wilds where no one could see us, I couldn't bear to have them looking like little ragamuffins. So beside all the other washing for the family there were fourteen gingham pinafores to wash every week—and fourteen pairs of white cambric drawers, which were white only once, and that was before the first wearing.

Those much-punished undergarments spent hours and hours astride the top rail of the corral—always a box seat for whatever was going on. By dint of much rubbing on the weathered poles the white drawers acquired a greenish grime which wouldn't come off, or in contact with a new pine pole they would pick up a lump of pitch. They took the brunt of it when the children rode bareback, the effects of a hot little body, a galloping horse, and a warm day being just what you would expect. I take off my hat to who-ever was bright enough to think of making bloomers for a little girl out of the same material as her dress. I wasn't bright enough, and by the time someone was, my children were grown.

A mother's life was harder then than now, for the lack of such simple things. There were no zippers, and no snaps which children could fasten themselves. When Fay and Mabel went out to play in the winter,

I would have to button up two pairs of jersey leg-gins, button by button, to the waist. Then when I'd done all that they would be back in no time at all, it seemed, with cheeks like apples and with eyes like stars, announcing that they'd had enough snow and wanted to play *indoors* now.

They were lovely little girls. Mabel kept her curls, and they both had blue eyes set wide apart, and long eyelashes. My mother loved beauty so, it was a pity that we did not live where she could have seen more of her little granddaughters. But I was so busy getting three meals a day, I don't think I ever realized they were pretty, until we moved to town where I saw them with other children.

I don't think there is anyone so unfitted to raise children as a tired mother, and I was always tired. And then too there were the effects of isolation and of living inside four walls. In the early days when I had only Mabel I could, even if rarely, pack her in the spring wagon and go on a day's trip with Mr. Alderson, or visit the roundup when it was working near. My sidesaddle was lost when the Indians burned our house, but once or twice on Tongue River I rode short distances on a man's saddle, knee crooked around the horn, while Mr. Alderson took the baby on a pillow in front of him. Two children, however, made all that a thing of the past, and later there were three, and then four! I've said there were weeks when I didn't leave the ranch. There were weeks, in our long winters, when I scarcely left the house except to hang clothes on the line.

No mother gives her best to her children under these conditions, and I know I wasn't patient with mine. But I religiously sang them to sleep every night, or read to them—though sometimes I was so tired I'd fall asleep myself in the middle of the story. I agree heartily with the modern parents and teachers who say that to do this is nonsense, and bad for the child, but at the time I thought I had to do it. They looked like such angels when they were tucked in bed, in their little white nightgowns, that sometimes I couldn't help saying: "Oh, why can't you be good children in the daytime, and not try me so?"

I remember Mabel's serious reply: "But Mother, we can't be good *all* the time!"

Yet with all my mistakes my children today, I am glad to say, look back to a happy childhood. They had more freedom than many modern children whose mothers know more of psychology than I did. And children thrive on freedom. Most of the time they were outdoors and away from me, living and learning for themselves. For hours they roamed at will, out of the range of "don'ts." When they did come indoors, though, I overworked "don't" until sometimes I myself wished that the word had never been invented. People have asked me since if, living in isolation, I didn't have an unusually close companionship with my children. I suppose I did—but I never noticed it! When you live so close to the bare bones of reality, there is very little room for sentiment.

Chapter XV

MUDDY, DESPITE ITS NAME, WAS BEAUTIFUL. TREES
were lacking, except the few pines on the hills, but
there was good grass in the valley and lots of springs
up the draws; and mornings when the sun was shining I would go to the door and see the white-faced
cattle coming down the hills to water. I had a good
garden patch on Muddy, and I worked in it steadily
during the warm weather. I think nothing helps a
woman so much as working in a garden, just because

it's outdoors. I had a good spring house too, and I'd wheel Fay down there in the baby carriage, and push her back up the hill with the butter and cream piled in front of her.

I got so tired of doing the same things every day —cooking and washing and ironing and making clothes for the children—that it was a real pleasure to fix up the house. There was a soft stone the Indians found in the hills that made an excellent whitewash; you could pound it up and pour water on it, and it would slack just like lime. I got them to bring me some of this rock, and I whitewashed the house that summer. To brighten it up indoors I took some old white blankets that had been worn thin, and dyed them red with diamond dyes; and I cut up an old wool lace shawl which I put round them for edging, and I made curtains out of those. Then I bought some red calico at the Indian store and made ruffled counterpanes to hide the ugly legs of our home-made beds; and the effect was so cheerful that the agency farmer, who married our Miss Roberts from Tongue River, came in one day and said it was the prettiest room he ever saw.

In one corner of the bedroom there was a place where the logs did not join properly, so I took a big straw hat I had and filled it with pine boughs and pretty grasses, and hung it over the rough spot. Mabel was extremely proud of this arrangement and would point it out to visitors, telling them how "Mama put it up there to hide the ugly place in the wall." We had a custom of lining the inside of a log house with cloth; on Tongue River we had used unbleached muslin, and white-washed over it. But on Muddy we thought we might as well be gay even if it did cost a little more. So after a year or two we covered the logs with cretonne. It stayed clean a long time.

All in all, the house was fairly comfortable, even if everything in it was homemade. We had been there a year when the county assessor came to see us one day, to place a value on our property for taxes. He was a nice man, just as kind as he could be, and when he came inside to appraise our furnishings, he told us that the county gave a two-hundred-dollar exemption on the contents of the house. But after he had looked over our homemade fixings piece by piece, and had figured up how little they came to, he was stumped. He said: "Why, Mrs. Alderson, you don't have a thing here except what you've made yourselves. I'd say the county owes *you* two hundred dollars."

How fast a new country changes! Ten miles away from us, at the site of the first Zook and Alderson ranch on Lame Deer, quite a community was springing up around the Cheyenne agency. The agent and his wife, Mr. and Mrs. Upshaw, lived in a very ele-

gant house made of frame, with carpets in every
room and plastered walls. They were fond of visitors,
and their home was a social center. Mr. Cox, the
boss farmer at the agency, had married Miss Roberts.
They lived with the Upshaws, and she taught the
Indian school. The teacher at the Rosebud school,
Mrs. Carpenter, also lived there, so there were three
women under one roof—a thing almost unheard
of.

Mrs. Upshaw was a refined, pleasant woman who
had never roughed it before. I remember her well
for her newcomer's point of view, so different from
that of myself, a hardening veteran of the frontier.
That spring when she came to visit us on Tongue
River, she had idealistic views about the Indians,
as fresh arrivals so often did. They came to our house
in droves, begging, and of course I fed them, but I
would simply put everything out on one big platter,
give them a few knives and forks and put the coffee
pot out. After watching them eat out of one dish
like this, she said one day, very sweetly: "Do you
mind if I treat them like white guests and try teaching them proper usage at table? I will wash the
extra dishes."

I told her of course to go ahead, and she set a place
neatly for each Indian. The experiment was a success
until the end of the meal, when the squaws simply
scooped up the leavings and tied them up in their

great full calico sleeves, to take home. One old woman even emptied out the coffee grounds and tied them up in the same way.

At the end of our first year on Muddy my teeth were troubling me badly—the start of a miserable siege which lasted for years. It was decided that I must go to Miles City to see a dentist, and we made quite an expedition of it. We took Brown and both the children, and Mr. and Mrs. Upshaw went with us. Our first overnight stop was the ranch of the two bachelor Robinson brothers. These men were a joy to stay with, they were such fussy housekeepers. No woman kept a neater house. But Mrs. Upshaw wasn't accustomed to western ways; she looked for white linen, and I had to smile to see her pin a towel over the clean calico pillow slip they gave her. For I knew that the Robinsons' was by far the nicest place we should have to stay in, this side of Miles City.

When we came to Rosebud station on the Northern Pacific, a dreary choice confronted us. Most travelers stayed at the section house, as it was called, one of the grim-looking shacks built at intervals along the railroad, to house the section hands and an occasional freight train crew. The section house was clean, but bare as a box car inside, and it was painted, like all of them, the unvarying box-car red.

The only other place to stay was a bachelor cow camp near by, and Mr. Alderson chose that because he knew he could get good care for the horses. We all slept in the one room. Mr. and Mrs. Upshaw had a real bedstead—but no sheets. There was no knowing who had slept in the blankets. The pillows were cased in flour sacks, which were none too clean. Mr. Alderson, Brown and Mabel slept in a roundup bed which they spread on the floor. The bunk bed which the baby and I occupied together was furnished with a straw tick and blankets, which evidently hadn't been used for a long time, because every time we turned over the dust flew up, and got in our noses. But it must have been clean dust, because it didn't hurt any of us.

Such experiences are not pleasant, and yet I do not think that they really harm people. It seems to me that when we are protected overmuch from dirt and discomfort we become overwrought in our attitude to such things; we fear them too much, and the fear hurts us more than the dirt and discomfort themselves.

We had one rattlesnake incident on the new ranch, while Fay was a baby. I had a pretty patch of lawn around the house. It was just the native wild grass that they call blue-stem, but we fenced it, and Mr. Alderson would lead one of the horses in once in awhile to crop it and keep it short. I had formed the habit of putting my dish towels out on this grass to bleach, and when it was time to bring them in I would wheel the baby out in her buggy, pick up the towels and pile them at her feet.

One afternoon I had finished gathering up my towels and had pushed the buggy up over the broad stone step into the kitchen. As it rolled into the house I heard that awful whirr of a rattlesnake. I stood frozen. The whirr was very close, and a thought of pure horror flashed through my mind; in picking up the clean towels I had picked up the snake and put it in the carriage with the baby! I could no more have moved a muscle than if I had been turned to stone.

Luckily our hired man, John Logan, was in the kitchen and he reached over and grabbed Fay up. Then, very carefully, he began taking out the towels one by one. There was no snake.

He said: "It must be under the floor boards. It probably crawled under the house during the heat of the day."

I said: "We've got to find it. I'll never have a moment's peace until we do."

We couldn't get under the floor boards, but after supper we made a search outside, hoping it had crawled out again. Still no snake. All next day I kept the children indoors, and the next, and you can imagine what an ordeal that was. On the evening of the second day, after they were in bed, thinking that the snake might have crawled outside in the cool of the evening, I was having another hunt in the grass, when I heard a whistle. It was Mr. Alderson, just in sight down the road. Oh, what a relief!

"What are you looking for?" he asked.

"A snake," I said.

"You haven't got snakes in your boots again, have you?" he wanted to know.

Well, we searched for another half hour and found the snake and killed it. And that was the only snake scare I had while we lived on Muddy.

Chapter XVI

ALTHOUGH WE KEPT A FEW OF OUR CATTLE ON THE
Muddy ranch, Mr. Alderson gave most of his attention from then on to raising horses. After we had
been there two years he took most of the money he
had realized from the cattle and bought a big bunch
of mares. He also bought a trotting horse stallion, and
for a time he planned on raising and training trotters,
even to building a trotting track around the oat field.
Unfortunately we were just entering a long slump

181

in horses, though we did not realize it at the time; no one seemed to want horses in the early Nineties; was the West raising too many of them? At any rate, it wasn't until the Boer war came along, with its immense demand for cavalry animals, that the horse market recovered. And that was too late for us.

The good and faithful Brown was still my husband's principal helper, but when he bought the mares he hired another boy, Billy Stanton, to help with the horse-breaking. Billy was a very good-looking cowboy who always wore the finest hats and the largest spurs, and handled horses with a good deal of dash. I am sure he was born too soon. He should have been in the rodeos or the movies. As it was, he left us about 1890 to go and hunt gold in Alaska.

We raised corn and oats for feed, and after our Kansas ranch hand, John Logan, decided to go and work as a farmer for the government, Mr. Alderson thought he would let the two cowboys do the ranch work—what people call farm work in eastern states. But it was a mistake to put cowboys to farming. They meant well, but all they did was break up a lot of machinery, especially Billy. Mr. Alderson finally decided it would be cheaper to hire a ranch hand, so he wrote to Minnesota and got Toby Larsen.

What a good boy he was! He was fresh from Norway when he came to us, having been in Minnesota only a year, blond and rosy-cheeked, and the best worker we ever had when it came to farming. Through him we brought several other Norwegian boys into our community, to work for neighbors. He was a faithful friend who was with us for years, long after the rest of them, even Brown, were memories. We lived so far away from people that those who worked for us loomed large in our lives, and Brown and Toby stand out. Brown was with us till the fall of 1892, and then we lost him, after nine years. He had been having spells of pain, so bad that they forced him to get off his horse. He would come to me after one of these spells and say: "Do you think I have cancer?" For his mother and his grandmother had both died of it.

What could I say except, "No, of course you haven't." But riding made him worse, so that fall, though only in his early thirties, he had to give it up, and he went back to Kansas to his people. Back there he bought a drug store, but he grew worse and died a year or so later, of cancer of the stomach. But that is getting far ahead of the story.

I have always hated a whiney woman, and I did succeed in keeping my lips shut tight over what I was thinking. But there were times when I couldn't keep from feeling sorry for myself inside. When this happened I would think of a neighbor of ours, old Mrs. Rowland, and try to learn a lesson in patience and cheerful living.

I called her our neighbor. She lived six miles down from us, at the forks of Muddy, with her husband and a delicate younger son. We had known her ever since we lived on Lame Deer; and when I could, which was not very often, I would hitch up my gentle driving horse to the dog cart, load the children in, and go and pay her a visit. The family came from Missouri and had quite a history. Her oldest son had run away from home when he was seven years old, and had gone to live with the Cheyennes, who were then in Indian Territory. He had learned their language and married a squaw, and he was now military interpreter for the government at Fort Keogh, outside of Miles City.

It was he, coming back to his mother after many years, who had brought them out here a few years before this and located them on a ranch. Mrs. Rowland was well along in years, and a cripple. She always made me feel ashamed of myself for ever venturing to think my own lot a hard one. For I at least was young when I came out to help conquer a new country. But Mrs. Rowland was old when all her home ties were broken, and she was brought out to spend the last of her days on this vast, little-settled frontier. She reminded me of a great tree, uprooted after she was old and planted out here among all these Indians.

Their shack was as neat as possible, neater than

mine, and the first I ever saw that was white-washed with that soft stone the Indians used. There she would sit, in one place except when her younger son pulled her chair from room to room; a tall old woman with fine eyes. I never saw her reading anything, and there was little work she could do. But she never complained, and she always seemed able to think of others and forget herself; she often said that her youngest son was so good to her, but that he had to work too hard. She seemed serene and happy under conditions which would have killed most people—her daughter-in-law just a blanket squaw, her only relatives, besides her husband and this younger son, a family of half-breeds. Her grandchildren were all handsome, as mixed-bloods often are, and they were a very nice family—but to her they must have seemed alien just the same. Just once she dropped the remark that her older son would have been better off financially if he'd had a white wife. For Indian in-laws had one very practical drawback, and this, no doubt, was what the old lady referred to. They would come and live off you if they could, and any white man, who fell a victim to the charms of a black-eyed Indian girl, was sure to have a huge tribe to support forever after.

One of the old lady's granddaughters, a striking brunette with a sun-tan complexion, had married a white man. They had two little girls, who were therefore three-quarters white. Regardless of fractions, they were charming children—and our children's only playmates. Every so often, Mr. Alderson would send a wagon the six miles down the creek to bring them up for the day, and Mabel and Fay just loved them. As Mabel said, "they can make such nice play houses." One day the father came, and brought our children a beautiful gray cat he had found straying in the hills.

We felt really close to that family. Just before Christmas one year the cowboys at our ranch saw a picture of a wheel chair in a Montgomery Ward catalogue. Someone said: "That's just the thing for the old lady," and they all chipped in and bought her one. Her younger son had to cut every door in their three-room house wider to let it through, but after that she could roll herself from room to room, and even outdoors.

One other person whom I knew at this time stands out unforgettably—Little Wolf, the Cheyenne chief. This Little Wolf had been a great leader, and his name is in a dozen history books—though his squaw did our washing. With Dull Knife, an older chief, he commanded the great march of his people in 1878, when they defied the orders of the government, left their reservation in Indian Territory, and struggled northward, men, women and children, determined to get back to their old home in Montana.

Until he surrendered at the end of that journey, Little Wolf had been regarded as one of the most dangerous of hostile Indians—though he always had a reputation for humanity and decency in his dealings with the whites. But after the surrender the Cheyennes were given a reservation up here, and Little Wolf was a leader in keeping the peace. For a time he was made chief of the Indian police by the military authorities at Fort Keogh. But when he killed an Indian he was trying to arrest, his tribe cut him off, and at the time we knew him he had no standing with his people any more, and no voice in their counsels. He was a pathetic figure of a deposed king, but there was a dignity about him, despite his poverty, that was touching. I was always convinced that despite his reputation as a chief who had bitterly fought the government, he had it in him to be a good American if only the "Great Father" could have been made aware of his great heart and his capacity to serve. He respected the order of the government against sun dances, in which the Indians imposed mutilations and bodily torture upon themselves to show their bravery, and when the members of his tribe near us disobeyed that order and held a sun dance, Little Wolf wouldn't allow his lodge to go. Some other Indians cut up his tepee and ran off his horses, to express their opinion of him.

Many a time I had seen him talking with Mr.

Alderson in the sign language, explaining his favorite view that "The Indians should be friendly with the white people, and after awhile they would get to be one big people"—making a great sweeping gesture with his arms. The sign language was so beautiful and eloquent that I hardly needed to be told what he was talking about.

Since moving to Muddy I no longer had Rattlesnake and Minnie to work for me, for we lived too far away. I needed another squaw to help me with the washing, and that was how we came to know Little Wolf. He had two squaws, and he brought the one he thought less of to wash for us. I always felt as though I had a nurse for the children the day he came. He would look around through the rocks for snakes before he would let the children sit down and play; and together they would climb the hills to hunt for pretty rocks for their play houses. Sometimes they would help Little Wolf gather kinnikinnic, a bark which the Indians used in place of tobacco. Little Wolf never begged nor stole, but his squaw was not so honest, and would sometimes make off with our towels. He would bring them back the next day, handing them to me and saying: "Squaw hypersiba," with such pathetic dignity that I was much moved.

We made him a present of a pipe, and he would hold it in his hands between smokes, rubbing it over and over in a pleased way and saying: "Heapie good, heapie good." In time the stem broke off, but for quite a while he kept us from seeing it, holding the thick part of the stub between his teeth—where any other Indian would have called our attention to it so we would give him a new one. Of course when we discovered it we did give him a new one.

When we decided to move away from the ranch and live in Miles City, and Little Wolf heard about it, his emotion was something I shall never forget. He just begged us not to go. He said: "Your papooses will get sick down in Miles City, maybe die, and I not see you any more." And tears rolled down his cheeks.

The papooses did not get sick in Miles City, but my husband was killed there, and they said that when Little Wolf heard about it he cried like a child. He would come to our old ranch and follow the people around, asking everyone to tell him about it, although of course he did not know English very well—and they said he never seemed satisfied until he understood how the accident had happened.

I myself have had no wide experience of such things, but a Montana neighbor of ours told me that Little Wolf's was the only case he had ever known of an Indian showing real affection for a white man; that is, as far as our part of the country was concerned.

When I reflect upon all the frontier folk that I have been associated with, I think the ones that made the most lasting impression on me were old Mrs. Roland, mother of the Agency interpreter, and Little Wolf, the war chief of the Cheyennes. They had one impressive trait in common; a quiet resignation to "the inevitableness of things." They had other like traits of character, too, despite their widely separated backgrounds—both were kind, both had courage, and both had a childlike interest in simple things—in the sunlight and the beauty out of doors. Each of them appeared happy under conditions that most people would regard as impossible, and it always seemed to me that theirs was the happiness which can only come from integrity and inner peace. Their example more than any other helped me to "keep my chin up" when things were hard. I don't want to be misunderstood; I wouldn't have exchanged my lot for that of any other woman on earth. But, perhaps just because the rewards were great, the going at times was proportionately rough.

Years after this when I was a widow living in Birney, Montana, Little Wolf would come twenty-five or thirty miles to visit me and my children every fall. He was a very old man by that time and blind, and his squaw would walk the whole distance leading his horse. She was the one we thought was "hyper-siba" because she stole our towels, but when we saw her devotion to the old man in walking that long way, we were reminded again what a mixed thing human nature is, and how often one is compelled to give admiration where one least expected to.

In 1889, Mr. Alderson bid on the contract to supply beef to the Crows and Cheyennes. He got the contract, and he bought several hundred head of cattle in Nevada that spring and shipped them in. But there was a slip-up on the terms of the deal, because his partner in Miles City had failed to specify that they were to be delivered all at once. So when Mr. Alderson arrived at Crow Agency with the cattle, the agent insisted upon his delivering them in small bunches weekly, till winter came. This meant hiring cowboys and holding the herd for weeks, and we just about went broke on it.

But while it was disastrous in a business way, it did make pleasure. For after his first trip over to Crow Agency Mr. Alderson said: "I shall have to be over there a long time, so you and the children might as well come over and stay." What an outing that was! The clerk at the agency, Mr. Barstow, was a splendid man with such a nice wife, and we went over and stayed in their spare bedroom and ate at the agency mess. It was a month's glorious holiday for me.

The doctor at the agency was a tall, light young

man with a good deal of presence, and I believe well educated; he enjoyed the country and would take the ladies driving almost every afternoon. It was late summer and the days were beautiful. No matter where we went on our drives, we would always wind up at the scene of Custer's last stand, above the Little Big Horn. There was a wonderful view up there, with the Big Horn mountains to the southwest and a long, low ridge to the west; and as we looked over the valley where the Sioux camp had been, we could almost see Custer's blue-coated troopers marching over the hills, on that terrible June morning. The two-hundred-odd men who died had been given a hasty and shallow burial by the troops who arrived on the spot a few days after. In later years they were taken up and placed in proper graves, but at the time I visited the scene, thirteen years after the battle, the bones had not been removed. The rains had washed them and the coyotes disturbed them, and in many places they were lying on the top of the ground, all scattered about. I picked up a little bone from a hand one day, and a link of a backbone. I had them a good many years before I gave them to somebody. I remember seeing the gold filling in a tooth on one skull.

While I was on the spot and soaking in memories of the old tragedy, I read Mrs. Custer's fine and womanly book, "Boots and Saddles." One thing she said impressed me particularly with its wisdom. She said that the army women on the plains learned never to say they were thirsty unless there was water there to drink; never to say they were hungry unless there was food. Which seemed to me to have a bearing on my own life.

I never told my mother, never even began to tell her, all the things I put up with on our last ranch. If I had she would have worried and would have said it was Mr. Alderson's fault. It was not his fault. He did the best he could. All those years he was trying to make money, but they were bad years when everything collapsed, and everyone in the country was hit the same way; and then there were individual misfortunes like that Crow Indian deal. Mother never understood the conditions of life out here. For instance, there was the time we gave our great party, before the Upshaws went away.

That was the time that all our friends came from over on Tongue River—they, and Mrs. Cox's younger sister Emma, who later married Lew Alderson, and a cousin who was visiting them—oh, it was a great occasion, and we had worked for days to prepare for it. Mr. Alderson had cleared a place outdoors and shoveled it down level, and we had two big canvas wagon sheets which we pegged down to make a dancing floor. Then the boys chopped down little pine trees on the hills, and planted them all around and hung lanterns on them; they were just plain farm lanterns, but it did look pretty. And the lighted windows of the house looked right out on the dancing space, and we put lights in there, too. There was no room in the two-room house to put all those people, so we reserved that for the ladies, and we fixed up the stable for the boys—because the horses were all out on the hills in the summer time. We cleaned it well, and put down fresh, sweet, new mown hay in the box stalls, with blankets and pillows, and it made a lovely dormitory.

The guests stayed two or three days, and I think they all had a good time. There was much that I held back in my letters home, but I was really proud of this party, so I wrote and told mother all about it, thinking she would be pleased to know how well we managed after all—even to entertaining nice people successfully—though we did live in a wilderness.

She wrote back: "My daughter, I can't understand how you can invite people to your house when you can't make them comfortable."

Chapter XVII

HARDLY ANYONE WAS EVER ILL IN OUR PART OF THE country. The climate was good, and disease germs were few. When someone wanted a doctor, it was usually for one of two reasons; an accident, or childbirth. Wanting a doctor was one thing, however, and being able to get him was quite another. My last two babies were born on the ranch, and I had no doctor for either. Patty, what's more, was born in the kitchen.

In the summer of 1890 I went home for one more visit to West Virginia, taking the little girls. There had been Indian trouble lately, and more was brewing. Mr. Alderson had to be away all summer, taking horses to Kansas to sell, in hopes of a better price. He did not want to leave me alone so he insisted upon my going home, but if I had known in time that Patty was coming, I might have arranged to postpone my trip, nevertheless. As it was, I couldn't possibly prolong my stay for so many additional months. In the fall, therefore, I returned to Muddy Creek, to think about having a baby, for the first time, on the ranch.

This time going to Miles City was out of the question. I couldn't go away and leave the two children —and it was equally impossible to take them. We looked at it from every angle and tried to see some better way out, but there was none. I would have to take my chances where I was.

For years the only doctor to be had in our part of Montana, nearer than Miles City on one side and Sheridan, almost as far away on the other, was the one kept by the government at Lame Deer for the Indians. We arranged to have him come to me when the baby was to be born. I don't know how good he was, but at least he was a doctor—and sober. Some of those who practiced out west in the early days spent most of their time in the clutches of the demon rum, having come here because they couldn't keep a practice back east. I heard of one such in another part of Montana, who was usually "rounded up" several days ahead of time by the relatives of the mother-to-be, and kept under lock and key to make sure that he would be on hand and sober when the time came.

The agency doctor was of a different type. He seemed a reliable young man, and I confess it was a blow when he told me that he was leaving the country. His father had died, and he was going home to Iowa to be with his mother. He rode over to break the news to me one winter day, seeming quite genuinely disturbed. He told me that he hated to leave me without care and had debated it a long time in his conscience, but had ended by deciding that his first duty was to his mother.

So, there was nothing to do but make the best of it. We engaged Mrs. Young, our neighbor from Muddy postoffice, to come up and stay with me. I was convinced in my mind that I should be all right, but a woman's feelings at such times are not always controlled by her mind. I became foolishly depressed, even morbid, before the baby was due. I felt that I was going to die, and I asked Mr. Alderson, if I did die, to take me in and bury me where there were water and flowers and trees, not one of these lonely hills.

He said he didn't feel that way about death. He wanted to be buried where he was, not carted around. He felt that when you died, it was just like throwing away an old coat. I knew he was right; yet I couldn't help shivering when I thought of those lonely graves out west, so far from friends. Every so often you would come across one all by itself on a hillside, just covered by a heap of stones, with a fence around to keep the cattle from trampling it. They had always seemed terribly forlorn to me.

All this was foolishness. Patty was born in April, quite successfully. It was the time of year when baby calves are beginning to show up, their little white faces so clean and new that they look like human babies; the time when the creeks are running full, and the mountains are dark blue and brilliant with melting snow, and the whole landscape is one of incredible brightness and rejoicing. I remember that earlier on the day of Patty's arrival, Mr. Alderson and Mrs. Young and I set out a strawberry bed.

We had built more onto the house by this time, adding a kitchen-dining room, a room for the children next to mine, and a big back porch with a root cellar right by. We used the old kitchen for our bedroom, and the new arrangement gave us a room to spare. People didn't tell children anything in those days, so when I felt that the baby was coming their father told them they were to sleep in the spare bedroom that night, without any explanations. But I never got any further than the hired boy's folding bed in the kitchen. It was our third little girl—but if Mr. Alderson was disappointed he never showed it. I never realized how much he had wanted a son, until Walter was born.

Later that night Mr. Alderson picked me up and moved me to my own bedroom. From there I could follow every sound in the kitchen, and recognize just how badly things were going without me! This experience brought home to me the vital necessity of a woman's being away from home when her baby is born. She can't rest in her own house, because she can't stand lying in bed when there are things to be done. In ten days I was up and doing all my work, as usual. I felt strong enough at the time, but I paid for it later.

I never had chloroform with any of my children except the one born in West Virginia. The old Kentucky doctor in Miles City didn't give it—I know no reason why. Long after I had had all my own children, I was told that in Birney the women kept chloroform on hand and learned to use it. Once, by means of it, they even saved a life.

They had sent for the agency doctor when this woman was expecting her baby; not the doctor I knew, but another, for this was several years later. They said he boasted of having nine diplomas, and was considered first rate, but when she had been in labor for a night and a day, uselessly, and they saw she would die like this, he confessed that he had never had a baby case before, and he fell on his knees and begged for forgiveness.

They sent a cowboy riding to Sheridan then, sixty miles away, for a doctor they knew to be competent; and during the fifteen hours that it took the cowboy to get there and the doctor to get back, those women kept her under and kept her pains stopped with chloroform. Without it she would have been dead before he arrived. The man they sent rode at a gallop without stopping, except to change horses; he rode into ranches and simply took what he found in the corral. No one would have refused a horse in such a case, but had anyone done so the horse would have been taken, at the point of a gun if necessary. On his way in he arranged relays of fresh horses for the doctor. He made the ride in six hours; the doctor, coming out, took eight or nine. Cousin Peachey Cox, who tells of all this, says that she never forgot the sight of the doctor's buggy coming over the hill, against the sunrise.

The baby was dead, but the mother lived and had four children.

The Birney community was an exceptional one. They were all fine, intelligent people, and there were so many women—four or five at least—that they looked after each other. But I was isolated. I never had the opportunity either to give or to receive such help. However, I was lucky. I always had what they call an easy birth.

When I had my last baby on the ranch, I knew from the start that there would be no doctor. The first one had never come back to the agency and had not yet been replaced—so the Indians, these last two years, must have been no better off than I was. But we did hear of a midwife down the creek. That is, she said she was a midwife. She was cooking and doing housework on one of the ranches, and her job was up in November, so, as we looked for the baby in December, she came to us right away. We found out later that she had not been on a baby case for at least seven or eight years, but at the time we were glad to get her, as Mrs. Young couldn't come.

She was a tall, gaunt old soul, uneducated, but fairly clean. She was helpful enough as far as the housework went. But she was homesick! She had a daughter and grandchild living down on the Yellowstone, and she did so want to be with them for Christmas—and Walter inconsiderately delayed his coming until January 6. She would come and sit with us in the evening after her work was done, and cry into her apron, night after night. I was having a wretched time with toothaches and was feeling depressed anyway, and she completed my misery. I told Mr. Alderson I'd almost as soon go through it alone as have her around.

And as it turned out I might better have been alone. For she was far too old and out of practice, and she lost her head when the time came. Walter was born in the cold and the dark of a winter's morning. Afterwards Mr. Alderson went out to do chores, and start the children's breakfast; and while he was gone the excited old woman let the fire go out in my room, and she bathed the baby in that awful chill, and we nearly lost him. When she brought him to me he was just like a little cold frog against my side. He caught an awful cold; and whether it was that or not I don't know, but for the first three months of his life he had terrible colic, and he cried and cried and cried.

Some time before all this, on his trip to Kansas in 1890, Mr. Alderson had bought two large, fine jacks and we were now raising mules. Our first mule colt, born in the spring of 1892, was quite an event in our household. The mother, a beautiful well-bred mare that the children claimed for their own, was driven in from the range when a late blizzard came up, for her baby was expected. The foal arrived on a bitter night, after the children were in bed, and Mr. Alderson brought it into the house and put it in one of my improvised clothes closets—a curtain hanging from a shelf.

When the children woke up next morning they were told to go and look behind the curtain, and there stood blinking at them our first baby mule. A mule colt is the cutest thing in all creation—not wobbly or ungainly like a baby horse, but a perfect little miniature of its full-grown self—and they were in raptures over it.

The morning Walter was born, Mr. Alderson told them again that he had something to show them after breakfast. During all the months since the arrival of the baby mule, they had never forgotten the thrill, and they were sure now that the surprise was going to be another little mule colt. Instead of that it was a baby brother.

How delighted they were! The two older ones printed a letter of announcement to their little friends on Tongue River, Albert and Joe Brown. It read: DEAR ALBERT AND JOE: WE HAVE A LITTLE BROTHER. HIS NAME IS WALTER. HE IS A BOY.

Not until I read that exultant last line did I realize how disappointed they, too, had been at not having a brother.

Taking the law of averages into account, we got off very easily during the years we lived so far from a doctor. We never had a serious illness. We had few accidents of the sort which occur so easily where men are riding and handling horses all the time. Terrible things could and did happen; it wasn't uncommon for a man's horse to fall with him, and he could lie out for a night with crushed ribs or a broken leg before he was found, sometimes in the dead of winter. With all that riding around and no means of communication, no one thought anything of it if a man didn't show up somewhere for hours after he was due. Western people were not apprehensive, and there was no undue haste in starting a search.

Once the man was found, he had somehow to be put back on a horse and packed to the ranch, or at least to a wagon road. Occasionally a litter would be made of a blanket stretched between two horses —but with the wild and unmanageable horses which those men usually rode, this wasn't simple either. Finally there was the problem of transportation to the doctor. All the ranches kept great sheets of surgeon's plaster with which to bind up a broken limb, and so save as much suffering as possible on the long, jolting journey. But that was about the only thing we knew in the way of first aid.

One of the few serious emergencies I can remember had me for its central figure. One summer, while we were living on Tongue River, I had a miscarriage when I was all alone except for a handful of well-meaning, frightened men. Mr. Alderson was away buying steers in Idaho, and I was at home with John, Zook, Brown, and some visitors. I had been feeling wretchedly for several days. One night, when I had put the baby to bed and was waiting for the house to settle down so I could go to bed myself, I went and lay down on the front porch.

Almost at once John came to me and said: "You're feeling badly, aren't you?"

I had to admit it. He was so dear and sympathetic. He said: "What you need is a hot toddy. You go to bed, and when you're all ready you call, and I'll bring it to you."

I accepted his offer gratefully, and after drinking the toddy I went into a deep sleep.

I woke up hours later terribly ill. Although I realized afterwards the danger I'd been in, I didn't stop to think of it at the time, and I wasn't frightened. I only knew I needed help. I lay there what seemed a long time, gathering my forces and waiting for daylight—for I knew I had strength enough to get up only once. When it was light enough to see, I got up and went to the drawer where the clean linen was kept, and straightened myself out as well as I could; then went to the door and called John.

When he saw me he looked scared to death.

He said: "Mrs. Alderson, you need a doctor." But the doctor was in Miles City, a hundred miles away!

I said: "I don't want a doctor. I want a woman!"

He went back to the bunk room across the hall to call the men, while I fell back into bed. I can still hear the thump of feet coming down out of those bunks, one after the other! Then John returned and said again that they wanted to go for a doctor. But I knew of a woman who had recently come in to work for some people down the river, and I told them to go for her instead. She was there by ten o'clock. I simply kept quiet and let her wait on me, and I recovered without any complications whatever.

I was always touched to see how, in the absence of women, men develop almost feminine qualities of thoughtfulness and sympathy. The men of those days, and especially the cowboys, could and did rise to the occasion when a medical emergency arose, and the best example of that I ever knew was Mr. Alderson. All those men, through their work with animals, developed a rough competence at surgery and care of the injured—but Mr. Alderson's wasn't rough. He had a natural sense of what to do when someone was hurt, and all the sympathy which ought to go with surgical instincts, but is sometimes conspicuously missing.

He saved the day when Mabel had her accident —the nearest thing to a bad one we ever had.

Mabel, then six or seven years old, was running outdoors when she fell, hitting her chin on a rock and biting her tongue almost in two. The end of it simply hung by a shred of flesh. We sent to Lame Deer to get help, but either it was one of our doctor-less periods at the agency, or the doctor, if there was one, was away. I know it turned out that our only chance of getting help was to send about twenty-five miles farther to the Catholic mission at Ashland, where Father Vandervelden was then in charge. We knew that the father had studied medicine before he entered the priesthood. The agent at Lame Deer sent an Indian horseback to get him, and Father traveled most of the night.

Mabel was hurt early in the afternoon and be-tween that time and the time Father Vandervelden reached us, which was well after sunup the next morning, Mr. Alderson took charge. The child was not in great pain after the first, but she was in mortal terror of the doctor, afraid that he would have to sew up her tongue. Her father slept with her that night, and every time she moved he would give her sips of milk to drink, and would remind her to be quiet and to keep her tongue still, telling her that if she did so, perhaps when the Father came he would not have to take stitches in it. He soothed her so that she actually did keep quiet and stop crying, trusting him. When Father Vandervelden arrived he said he couldn't have done any better if he had been there himself. The tongue had started to knit; no stitches were necessary; and a little girl's faith in a miracle-working father was happily justified.

In all the years of our life on a ranch, we never

had a doctor for the children but twice—counting Father Vandervelden as a doctor. On one of my visits east, a friend in Kansas had given me a little kit of homeopathic remedies to take home to the ranch, saying he had raised his family on it. I certainly raised mine on it. The kit contained a number of bottles of little white sugary pills, and a book of directions telling you which to use in case of colds, fever, stomach trouble and so forth. Whenever one of the children was ill I simply consulted the book and gave a pill from the proper bottle. The little pellets all looked and tasted alike, but either they were very potent, or the children had excellent constitutions, for they always speedily recovered.

Chapter XVIII

I ALWAYS FELT THAT I PERSONALLY HAD A GREAT
deal to be thankful for. I was healthier than the
average woman. I never had anything the matter
with me during all those years of living so far from
a doctor, except headaches and that everlasting
trouble with my teeth.

I had suffered from neuralgia all my life, as my
mother did before me, but I was much better out
here in this high, dry climate than I had been in

West Virginia where it rained a great deal. In the South I wore thin slippers regardless of the damp; out here I wore sensible shoes and overshoes, and the headaches troubled me much less—though they were very severe when they came.

I remember one of these attacks for the light it throws on the faithfulness of our Norwegian boy, Toby. It was early fall, and Mr. Alderson was away, and I had been having one of my sick headaches all day. So after his work was done Toby rode the ten miles down the valley to Muddy postoffice—making a round trip of twenty miles—"to see if there's a letter for you from Mr. Alderson." He came back four hours later, to report that there was no letter, but that he had found two baskets of purple Concord grapes that a friend had sent me. He had ridden back the ten miles with one wire-handled basket over each arm. You can imagine how good those grapes tasted after my day of headache; they were cold from the night air, and Toby and I sat up together and enjoyed them. I have remembered them all these years; I never knew anything that went so to the spot; but of course fresh fruit, except wild plums, was a rarity to us. Undoubtedly the remoteness of our life made us rather simple. To people living as we did, little things could give an almost piercing pleasure.

My troubles on Muddy, the worst ones, had nothing to do with bodily aches or pains. Instead I was haunted by a demon of fear. I can't remember when it began to grow on me, but I know that until I lived on Muddy I had never been afraid except those few times I was left alone. For the most part I never had sense enough to be scared, even when there was something to be scared of, such as a tribe of hostile Indians all around us. But now I was nervous about one thing or another all the time. The stallions were a source of constant worry to me, though until then I had never been afraid of a horse in my life.

I wasn't afraid for myself nor for the children, since we seldom went near them; but I was terribly fearful that one of them would hurt Mr. Alderson; or that they would break their halters, get loose in the stable and get together. This became an obsession with me. Yet suppose they *did* fight?

Mr. Alderson took the sensible attitude. He said: "Don't worry about it. If those studs ever do get together, just don't you try to separate them."

At different times during the years he was raising horses, we used different sires, but at the time I speak of there were two stallions on the place, and the two jacks. Both of the former were of draft-horse breeds; one, a brown one, was a Belgian; the other was a gray, and I think must have been a Percheron, though I am not sure. The brown was just as gentle and kind as he could be, but the gray was a mean animal—

so mean that Mr. Alderson never rode after him in the pasture without taking a six-shooter. And they were both such great, powerful creatures that the thought of their getting together and fighting was a terror to me.

I had real grounds for this anxiety. We had no box stalls at the time, only open stalls in which they were tied. One day one of the boys, through carelessness, buckled the halter of one of them too loosely, and he would have slipped it and been free in another moment, if Brown hadn't just happened to go back into the barn.

Finally it did happen, this thing I dreaded, and I was there to see it. It was when the men were building the box stalls at last. The stallions were outside, in opposite corrals. And on the same impulse, as it seemed, the two great horses made a rush and each one broke through his gate at the same instant as though it were pasteboard. They met in the center, where they reared and fought like bloodthirsty wild beasts or like the horses in nightmares, pawing and tearing at each other's throats. The men were all there, with axes in their hands, but it seemed minutes before they could stop them. Before the battle was over the ugly gray had whirled and kicked, and the brown who was gentle to humans had caught the other's pastern in his teeth and had bitten clear through the tendons, leaving him a cripple for the rest of his life.

It was an awful thing to see. I was more afraid than ever that it would happen again, when I was alone. I was afraid for Mr. Alderson, too, being around those fierce creatures; so much so that when he was out in the barn looking after them, if he stayed too long I'd go out to see if anything was the matter, and he would call out, "I'm all right."

And yet when the real trouble came to us through horses, later on in Miles City, I had put all that out of my mind.

Perhaps it was being alone so much that made things work on my imagination. Were other women on lonely ranches as foolish as I? I know that the worst ordeals I suffered were nearly all in my own head, and some of them, viewed afterwards, were funny.

I remember one morning I woke up with one of my headaches. It must have been worse than usual, because Mr. Alderson offered to stay home and look after me, instead of going back to the roundup— "unless," he added, "you'd rather have me go and take the children, so you won't have to bother with them."

The second plan sounded like a godsend. After they had left I lay down on the bed with my head throbbing, thinking what a blessing it was that I didn't have to get any meals. After awhile my head felt better and I got up, intending to start a little fire in the kitchen and make myself a cup of tea. I was out at the woodpile gathering chips, when I turned, and was startled nearly to death—for there behind me was an uncouth, bearded man, on foot!

Considering the way we took in every stranger who came to us on horseback, trusting him with all we had without a moment's hesitation, it may seem odd that I should have been frightened half out of my wits, merely because this man was walking instead of riding a horse. But everyone who lived in our part of the country felt the same way. If a man came horseback, he might be a horse thief or a murderer, but at least you knew he'd be a gentleman. On the other hand some very queer characters had gone through the country on foot.

I asked the man what he wanted, and he said he was looking for work. I told him that the foreman was down the creek, and that he should go down there to make inquiries. Then I asked him if he didn't want something to eat—because that was the law with us. He said he did, and I cooked him a dinner with my husband's six shooter and belt buckled on under my apron. No, he was not the type who would offer to help with the cooking.

When he had gone I took off that heavy old gun

and tried to rest again, but as soon as I closed my eyes I started imagining things. The man now knew that I was alone; he might be hanging around instead of going to see the foreman; what mightn't he do? I got up once more, and took Mr. Alderson's straight razor and tucked it into the front of my corset.

At about four-thirty my day of rest, such as it was, was terminated by Mr. Alderson, who came home bringing the children, and a man from the roundup. The bearded stranger came back too, with Toby, and I got supper for all of them, forgetting the razor, which was still tucked in my corset. Fortunately the poor fellow had left when it started popping up in the neck of my dress. Mr. Alderson wanted to know: "What's that?"

When I told him, he said I reminded him of the darky who kept two razors—asked why two, he explained that one was to shave with and the other was for social purposes.

I was always good at conjuring up the horrible things that *might* happen. But in the summer of 1889 we had a serious Indian scare, with fair prospects of a wholesale uprising and attempted massacre of the white settlers. And then, when there was real danger, I wasn't afraid.

A certain Crow medicine man fasted and saw a vision that now was the time for the Indians to join together and exterminate the whites. He tried to get the Crows to follow him and also the Cheyennes, but while the tribes as such hesitated to join, he gained a dangerous following of restless spirits among his own people.

My husband was in Nevada buying cattle when he saw from the newspapers that trouble was brewing, and wired some friends to go get the children and me and take us to Miles City. They wired back that the danger had been greatly exaggerated. Meanwhile I had heard that some of the Crows wanted to go on the warpath. But as I knew that the Crow tribe had a history of friendship for the whites—they had been our allies during the Custer campaign—I felt no anxiety and dismissed the matter from my mind. So I was very much surprised when Mr. and Mrs. Young came up the ten miles from Muddy postoffice to take us home with them for safety. Some of the Crows were already in open outbreak, and Mr. Young was "keeping his hand on the Cheyenne pulse," he said, through older, level-headed Indians who were friends of his. What everybody feared was that the Cheyennes would join.

We left in the afternoon. I packed our clothing quite calmly, and told the boys to turn out the blooded stock in case of danger and drive them as far away from the ranch as possible. They would be much better off at the ranch without me and the children to look after, and they kept up fast saddle horses in case they needed to make a getaway. It was after dark when we reached the Youngs. The long, pleasant living room where we had visited many times, with its bright curtains and big fur rugs on the floor, was full of men, and their guns lay loaded on the piano. No one showed any signs of alarm. Most of the men were neighbors, and we all chatted pleasantly.

Mr. Young, a typical frontier trader, heavy-set and bearded, was on the alert. He kept his ear trained outside, and when we heard the sound of horses galloping he would go to the door and hail the riders in Cheyenne. All the white people were indoors; some of those who galloped by were Crow scouts going to or returning from the Cheyenne camp, and others were Cheyennes. Those who stopped to answer Mr. Young told him that the Cheyennes weren't going to fight, and we began to feel reassured.

I hadn't undressed the children, but they slept soundly in the bedroom, and I never felt that sickening fear I had known when there was no danger. All night we sat listening for hoofbeats along the road and covering our thoughts with small talk. The day of wholesale scalpings and burnings, of babies brutally murdered and women raped, was over even then in our country; but how were we to know that?

Toward morning Mrs. Young and I went out and got breakfast for the rest of them, and with daylight we all felt better. Next day or the day after we learned that there had been a clash between the federal troops and the Crows, and the medicine man had been killed. And that was all there was to the outbreak.

But we did have a narrow escape that night, the children and I. For while we were at the Youngs', my brother-in-law Lew Alderson, who was foreman at the OD ranch, became anxious for us, and not knowing that we had gone, he and some other men arrived at the ranch at midnight bent on our rescue. Thank heaven, we escaped that rescue! For they had a plan to take us, not north toward Miles City, but south to Sheridan, Wyoming, over country much wilder and roads that were hardly roads at all. It was a perfectly good plan from their point of view —because to get to Miles City we should have had to go right through the Indians. But going the other way, to Sheridan, we'd have had to take roads that, to my way of thinking, were worse than any Cheyennes.

No modern, civilized person can possibly comprehend what the roads of those days were like— even the good ones. They were washed-out, narrow and full of rocks that jolted the teeth out of our heads; they hung over the edge of precipices; they were so steep that you almost fell backwards out of the wagon going uphill, and almost fell over on the horses' rumps going down. One time we were going on a visit to the Browns', over the well-traveled Tongue River road, and when we were crossing a wash at the bottom of a gully, the bump catapulted Patty out of the wagon—hurling her head *through* the spokes of the wheel! Mabel with great presence of mind jumped down and pulled her out. Luckily the team was gentle and we could hold them.

With such pictures in the back of my mind, you can imagine how Lew Alderson's scheme of rescue would have appealed to me. To have been packed into a wagon and started out in the middle of the night, into an unknown, almost trackless part of the country, with two small children, heaven knew what horses and perhaps a strange driver—well, I'd rather have faced the Indians.

Chapter XIX

THERE WAS AN OLD AND RATHER BRUTAL SAYING out west, to the effect that this was a great country for men and horses, but hell on women and cattle. Without going into the latter part of that statement, I should like to amend the first part. It was a great country for men and children. Especially for children.

Mine spent a fair share of their lives on their favorite perch at the corral, watching a show which to them was a rodeo and circus combined. When the men weren't away riding, something was always going on in the corrals. There were calves and colts to be branded, young horses to be halter-broken, saddled for the first time, and ridden, with frequent eruptions of bucking. The clash of man and horse on these occasions is sheer drama which never grows stale—and children love drama as much as grown people do.

Every now and then some horse with a wire cut that had become infected would have to be roped and thrown and "doctored." In the spring, before the roundup started, the whole saddle horse band would have to be shod; in the fall before they were turned out on the range the shoes would have to be pulled off again; and these routine-sounding operations, when performed on half-wild range horses, were not as they appear in peaceful pictures of the village smithy. The horses would snort and rear and kick, and often would have to be thrown before the shoes could be put on or taken off. There was endless suspense in watching the maneuvers of Mr. Alderson and Brown as they stayed out of reach of the desperate hoofs and finally brought the horse to do their will. No wonder the children loved the top rail of the corral! They would sit up there for hours, only climbing down long enough to fetch water for their father and the men to drink, or to run and tell me when something especially exciting happened. And I was up there on the rail with them in spirit, far more than in the kitchen peeling potatoes or baking bread.

The children learned a lot of things that I couldn't teach them. They did *not* learn manners or vocabulary. But they did learn from nature and animals. An Easterner who stayed with us once spoke of the difference he had noticed between our children's raising and his own.

He said: "You know, western children are more self-reliant and smarter than city children. They can look after themselves earlier, and they know so many things about life that city children don't learn until later—and then learn the hard way."

It's true that a ranch upbringing has one great virtue; it brings home the laws of life to children through nature, and at an early age, so that they have none of the curiosity which, I can well remember, tormented me when I was little. The summer I went home for my third visit, when we had the Indian scare out here, I remember telling Mother that I was afraid my four-year-old Fay would shock the Virginians by her candid horse-breeding talk. In those days Southerners were so modest that they wouldn't even refer to a bull by his right name. When they couldn't avoid mentioning him, they called him a "gentleman cow."

Mother replied: "I hope she does shock them. I have no patience with this mock modesty."

Highty-tighty as she was in some ways, she was very much more modern than the people around her.

My children had so little human companionship that their world was peopled with animals. Fay thought of nothing but horses, and had a herd of stick horses, on which she galloped around from morning till night. Our hired man used to say that you couldn't pick up a stick within a mile of the ranch that Fay wouldn't immediately classify as a "mare" or a "filly" or a "gelding" or something else, and add it to her herd. The stick horses had to be rounded up daily, corralled, driven to water, and fed on little piles of grass. She led the dog around by a halter, and any cowboy who sat down to visit in our house would be likely to find his legs all done up in bandages—as Fay had seen her father bandage the legs of the trotting horses—before he noticed what was happening to him. Fortunately the men in our country seemed to like children, and submitted patiently.

Mabel had different tastes. She was always a little housewife, and she learned very early to set the table and help me with the dishes—standing on a box to dry them. She liked to play house, and Lady-come-see, and the only way she could coax Fay to join her was by having a tea party, with something real to eat. But they were in complete agreement when it came to watching the work in the corral, or to riding their pony, Black Wolf.

The history of Black Wolf was one more chapter in the curiously mixed-up relationship between ourselves and Black Wolf, the Indian, whom Hal shot, and who caused the burning of our home. One day while we were living on Tongue River, the old Indian came to us leading a mare with a colt, which he wanted to trade By signs he explained that the colt was just the same age as the papoose—Mabel—who was then a few months old. We traded my little mule for them, and decided to break the colt for a saddle horse for the baby. We wouldn't let anybody but Brown ride him, so as to be sure to break him gentle, and as he was black we named him Black Wolf.

As long as he lived he was a much-loved member of the family. He was one of those perfectly gentle horses who seem to understand children, even to regard them as another species of colt. Since geldings will often show a real attachment to a little colt, even to adopting one which has been orphaned, there is nothing fanciful about the comparison. Black Wolf would stand with endless patience through their struggles to climb up on his back. When they were riding without a saddle this was a real problem, but the children solved it by waiting till he lowered his head to graze. Then one of them would straddle his neck; Black Wolf would toss his head up—not so much in protest as because he knew what was expected of him—sliding the child onto his back, facing his tail. Then she would turn around, and the next one would get on the same way.

He never threw the children but once. That time Mabel and Fay were riding him bareback; they took him down to the creek to water with another horse; when the other horse wheeled suddenly Black Wolf wheeled too, and off they both slid. They came to the house boohooing and protesting that "it wasn't Black Wolf's fault!"

We took him with us when we moved to Miles City, and a year or two later he ran off. He had always shown a violent liking for certain ranches near his old home, and I felt sure he was headed for a certain one near Birney, but as it was seventy miles away we did not go after him. Custom dictated the return of lost horses to their owners when recognized, but Black Wolf, though well known in that country, was not returned. For a winter the children there rode him to school, racing him through the bitter cold till he was lathered, and then letting him stand outside, so that he was badly crippled up with rheumatism the rest of his life. Later someone saw him and brought him back to us. We had him still when we moved out on another ranch some years later. Finally he got so that he couldn't eat from old age, and we decided one day, very reluctantly, that he would have to be shot. Next morning we found him lying dead by the haystack. He was twenty-two years old.

Our children saw so few people on the ranch, outside of the family, that a visitor was a great event, and they would follow him around without a moment's let-up and chatter at him until he was worn out. Women visitors were still more of a novelty, so the little girls tagged after them even more, and thought them all beautiful. Mr. Alderson said that our children never even allowed a guest a necessary moment's privacy—but they were so happy in the chance to talk to a stranger that I hadn't the heart to discipline them.

One time I remember a man came to the house, and the children had gone through their regular routine. They had escorted him around the place, and shown him their pets, and asked him if he had any little girls at home; and I don't doubt that Mabel had pointed out the basket hiding the ugly place in the wall; when she wound up by asking him gravely:

"Have you got any bedbugs at your house?"

He said, "No." (I think he was telling me a story.)

"Well," she said, "Mamma says *we* have enough for six families."

Yes—it was all too true. Those log houses with their numberless cracks were terrible places for harboring bedbugs. Since we had to put up with visitors of all kinds and descriptions, it was hard to keep the pests from getting in occasionally, and once they got in, you had to burn the house down to get rid of them. We acquired them when we had been on Muddy only a few months. A young man came to us, straight from staying in a bunk house which people said was just terrible. They soon turned up in his bunk in the kitchen, and from then on until we moved away six years later I fought bedbugs year in and year out. It was a hopeless struggle; the powerful chemicals of today were unknown, and the only defense was to blow a supposed disinfectant powder into the cracks.

This was what Mabel meant when she further explained to the visitor, with gestures, that "Mother goes *puff, puff, puff* all day."

People endure what they must, but I must say that of all the greater and lesser trials which afflicted us, bedbugs were the hardest to endure.

Except when the little Rowlands came to spend the day; and except for that great occasion, the visit exchanged twice a year with their friends, little Albert and Joe Brown, my children had no other children to play with. They had few toys, and no material advantages. But there were compensations. They did have pets—and I think that to most children animals are as important as people.

A ranch is a hospitable place. It has room for

everything, as for everybody. Neither man nor beast is turned away. It seems to me that at one time or another we harbored just about every representative of the four-footed kingdom that is found in Montana. The children were told they could have any kind of pet they wanted—except a lamb.

In view of the pets which they *were* allowed to have, this may seem an odd prohibition. One time Packsaddle Jack brought them two wolf pups which he had found in a den in the rocks—not coyotes, but real timber wolves, the deadliest killers of the plains. They were then only little snarling balls of gray fur. We shut them up in the corn crib, where they refused all food till they must have been almost starved. One morning one of the boys left the door open and one got away, and we turned the other one loose later—after all, it didn't seem right to kill a guest. We hoped, however, that our neighbor stockmen wouldn't hear of it, or at least that the government wolfer would catch him before he got big enough to do damage.

Another time somebody captured a fawn, which we fed on a bottle until he was old enough to eat grass. Eventually he grew up into a full-sized young buck, and was rather a dangerous pet. One day when Fay was playing with him at a little distance from the house he butted her down, and began pawing at her with his sharp little hoofs. We were all outside, for it was a beautiful summer Sunday, and Mr. Zook was visiting us with his bride. When he saw what was happening to Fay he took a rifle and shot the deer from on top of her. Except for a cut on the back of her neck she was none the worse—but was very indignant at her rescuer.

Since that was the kind of pet the children had, why the ban against anything so harmless as a lamb? The answer was that my husband was a cattleman, and hated sheep. There were plenty of them in the country—too many to his way of thinking—and pet lambs were easy to get, since they were always being orphaned and given away. But in our house a pet lamb was absolutely barred, and this, coming from so mild-natured a man as my husband, shows the strength of the feeling at that time.

However, on a trip to Crow Agency one time he found two goats, which he brought home as the next best thing. Mabel gave hers away but Fay kept the other one, and for the children's Christmas that year we ordered a little red cart and a patent leather harness from Montgomery Ward. The vehicle was elegant, but the goat refused to travel except down hill. However, by dint of much pushing and pulling, and twisting his short tail, they would get him to the top; then Fay would climb in and start throwing rocks, and the down grade would be made in a hurry. We kept him several years, taking him eventually

to Miles City, where we tied him up in the barn.
But it took all the boys and girls in the neighbor-
hood to keep him home even part of the time, as
he'd chew up anything he was tied with and run off
to Judge Brown's livery stable, where there was
another goat. We finally gave it up, and presented
him to Judge Brown for keeps.

We had been getting the Montgomery Ward catalog since 1885. It is impossible to exaggerate the
importance of the part played by this book of wonder
in the children's lives. They pored over it endlessly;
before they could read the pictures were there to
dazzle them, and as they made and revised their
shopping lists, a process which took weeks, they would
bring the book to Mr. Alderson or me to ask: "How
much does this or that cost?"—if the article was to
be a gift for one of us, holding their hand over the
picture. The catalog is well named "the wish book"
by country people.

In time they learned to spell out words in it. They
never went to school until we moved to Miles City,
when Mabel was almost ten years old. All they knew
up to that time was reading, as taught by Montgomery Ward, and printing block letters, which I
taught them. I never tackled arithmetic, but I had
an excuse; I'd heard that teaching methods varied,
and that teachers would really rather start their

children from the beginning than have them half taught or taught all wrong by their mothers.

The catalog came in the fall, and from then on they were blissfully busy making their plans for Christmas. They could change their minds every day as to what they would buy, just so their order was ready by the time their father went to Chicago with the cattle. Then he went to the firm, bought a cheap packing trunk, and patiently filled every child's order; then brought the trunk back with him on his railroad ticket. What a time when the trunk was opened!

On Christmas Eve we had a tree. The few store-bought ornaments were a thrill, but there was still more pleasant excitement attached to the cookie horses—our inevitable horses!—which the children cut out, baked, and branded in our brands with colored icing; then hung on the tree. The Christmas picture I remember best is the one made by Patty, just before she was two years old. She was dressed up in a red velvet dress which had belonged to my cousin Fanny in Atchison and been handed down to us. It had been worn by Mabel and Fay before her, and had finally been cut down to Patty's infant size. She remembered no other tree, and was kept out of the room till it was all ready to be lighted. Then, as one candle after another winked into flame, she hitched her little home-made rocker closer and closer till she was right under the branches of the tree, and her eyes kept getting bigger and bigger. That was the same Christmas we had the homesick old woman with us, and I was looking forward to Walter's arrival rather apprehensively. How closely happy memories and less happy ones are intertwined!

The children's best clothes were all hand-me-downs. Mabel was sixteen years old before she had a dress made of new materials. But my best talent was for making over old clothes, and they never minded at all. Their father taught them to be appreciative and they were really darlings; they would brag of me to visitors, saying with artless pride: "Look what Mother made us out of Mrs. So-and-so's old dress!" And they would point out what nice material it was —much nicer than we would buy if we bought new.

I was lucky, my friends in Kansas sent me such good things. A friend of mine in Miles City had a daughter who was a year older than Mabel, and I'd send them to her first, and then my children would wear them, one after the other. At that they were the best-dressed children anywhere around us. Dress goods seem to have been woven to last, in those days.

Mr. Alderson was a loving and patient father. Often he would come in dead tired from a long ride, and would lie down and sleep—with the children climbing all over him.

And he was wise. The little girls had a dog whom

they called "Dude"—having heard the word for the first time on the day of his arrival, and being impressed by it. Dude one day was indiscreet enough to tease the jack, barking and nipping at his heels as he stood in his box stall—and the jack bit him and almost cut his tail in two. The children wept and wailed over it, until Mr. Alderson told them they could go get whips and punish the jack. On the ranch we kept a couple of long bull whips, the kind used by cowboys in driving cattle. They have a long lash which cracks like a pistol shot when the whip is swung around your head—but it is quite an art to wield it. As the children didn't know how, their feeble pops bothered the long-eared criminal no more than a fly would, so it was a most effective treatment in the situation. They swung the whips, wore themselves out and relieved their feelings—and didn't hurt the jack.

Mr. Alderson was skilled in animal surgery, and he sewed up Dude's tail so it was almost as good as new.

Winter, in spite of its cold and snow, was my favorite season, for outside of a few horses and cattle to feed, Mr. Alderson's work was around the ranch and he was home most of the time. One year he even built a big bobsled in the kitchen. He worked only on parts of it at a time, but the chopping and planing, and boring and hammering, were music to the children and me. There was no being out for hours after he was expected home—hours which seemed endless, because I imagined all sorts of horrible things that might have happened.

If winter was the time of companionship, summers were lonely, and I have a memory of warm, empty afternoons with all the men away, and the children out playing, and only the buzzing of flies for company. But there was a kind of a peace, too, about those afternoons, and I would sew or iron in perfect contentment. I always felt safe about the children, and didn't worry about them as I did about Mr. Alderson. Despite our one snake scare I felt no apprehension about snakes near the house, as they were most unlikely to cross our green alfalfa patch; and the children weren't allowed to cross the creek and play in the dry, sunburnt hills unless Little Wolf was with them. Horses didn't worry me either, for the only one we ever allowed them to ride was good old Black Wolf. There at the ranch they seemed as secure as any child can be from accident.

Yet on one such peaceful afternoon Fay disappeared.

Patty was a baby at the time, and Fay not over four years old. And, as they say, she turned up missing. Mabel and I had a hunt for her. We found no trace, and then, from looking in the likely places, I turned to looking in the ones I didn't like to think about. I looked down the well, and in the stallions' box stalls. I looked in the pig pen where the old mother pig grunted over her young—for pigs are often vicious and have been known to attack and eat small children. I roamed over the place, calling, calling, calling, and wondering as I did so if some Indians had passed through the ranch that afternoon and picked her up. Then I went back into the house and started to search all over again in the places I had searched before. Mabel was a devout child. She now got down on her knees and prayed: "Dear God, please make us find Fay quick."

Never have I known such a dramatic demonstration of the power of prayer. All this time Fay had been hiding in a patch of big high thistles and ragweeds at the corner of the pigpen, where we could have touched her—she had a naughty, rebellious habit of not answering when I called. Just as Mabel finished her prayer, a bumble bee, which had been dining off a thistle, flew down and stung Fay's face, and she let out the most piercing war whoop ever heard.

The relief was great, but I spanked her anyway.

Chapter XX

I HAVE ALWAYS THOUGHT THAT FEAR IS OUR GREAT-
est sin. It shows such a lack of faith. It comes between
us and the light; it keeps us from doing things. All
of this and much more seems to me to be expressed
in the words of the Bible: "Perfect love casteth out
fear."

My love and faith were evidently a long way from
perfect, for during the years I spent on Muddy I was

afraid most of the time. Once the stallions were safely in box stalls and I didn't have any excuse for worrying about them any more, I began to worry about the Indians.

I don't think I was naturally of a nervous disposition. I think I was overworked. I had four children to care for with practically no help; I had gotten up too soon and had done too much work after the last two of them were born; I was worn out, and once more took to feeling sorry for myself. One thing, I am sure, that contributed to my unhealthy state of mind was the constant, nagging misery with my teeth.

Certainly toothache is not one of the major afflictions visited upon mankind, but there is one thing to be said for most of the woes that *are* major; they are soon over. Toothache goes on. For five or six years, after my children started to come, I had every kind of wretchedness that teeth are heir to. Mine were neglected because I was so far from a dentist. In time I came to have an obsession of unattractiveness because of them, so much so that I wouldn't even kiss the children. Mr. Alderson thought I was undemonstrative. He did not understand the real reason.

When you can't have your teeth properly attended to, there is only one thing to do, and everyone does it. You wait until one of them is aching so badly you can't stand it another minute, and then, when the prospect of having it extracted without an anesthetic is preferable to more of this torture, you go and have somebody pull it out. One time before Patty was born, when I had been up for two or three nights with the toothache, I finally went over to the agency to see if the doctor there could help me. He was away. But when I stopped in at a friend's house, holding my swollen jaw, I met one of our neighbor stockmen, who said earnestly: "Mrs. Alderson, you're suffering so, I wish I could do something to relieve you. I've never pulled a tooth in my life, but I'll try."

So we went to the doctor's office, where he picked out a pair of pliers. The poor young man! He was a Southerner, from Mississippi, and had always before been as jolly and full of fun as he could be. But at the prospect of this ordeal he was quite shaken. Before the operation, he braced himself with a toddy, and I followed suit. Then he did his best to extract the tooth. But it was a back tooth, and hard to reach; with the result that the forceps slipped off it—and knocked the filling out of the one above!

We let it go at that, as neither one of us was anxious to repeat the experiment. Strangely enough, the tooth stopped aching. I suppose the slight pull that he gave must have relieved it. But I was little better off, for soon afterwards the one which had lost its filling started to ache.

A year or two later I had one more such gruesome experience of amateur dentistry, that to this day I feel as though I would rather have a leg cut off than a tooth out. Patty was a baby, and again I was suffering with the toothache so terribly, that although it was the middle of haying time and Mr. Alderson was at his busiest, he decided that he would have to help me.

Fortunately we had a pair of dentist's forceps, which he had sent for so he could pull the children's first teeth. Word spread around the country that he had the instrument; he gained quite a reputation as a dentist, and people would come to him from miles away and beg him to pull their teeth for them. I remember one man who rode forty miles.

It was a hot July day when I had my ordeal, and I could see the men working down in the meadow.

Mr. Alderson came to me and said: "Now when you see me starting in with the next load of hay, you take a good, stiff toddy, and I'll pull that tooth."

I did as he told me. When he came back to the house he asked anxiously: "How do you feel?" But I was in such pain that the toddy hadn't affected me at all.

Then he said: "You'll have to take another," and he mixed me the biggest one I have ever seen. We both sat and waited for it to take effect. The curious thing was that I had never liked anything intoxicating to drink, with the single exception of that little California cordial in Miles City. I had never cared for wine, and had touched whisky only in cases of dire necessity; yet the second toddy didn't affect me either. I refused to let Mr. Alderson make me a third, and he went ahead. I took hold of the bottom of a kitchen chair and hung on, and he gave a pull which almost lifted me up standing, and then it came.

I remember saying: "Oh, I'm so glad that tooth is out!" And after that I didn't know another thing until four o'clock the next morning.

I woke up with my head feeling the size of a bushel basket, and all the unpleasant sensations which went with it. I didn't get up at all the next day, and at noon my tall, blond brother-in-law, Lew Alderson, came riding by with another man, riding the range. They stopped for dinner, and afterwards they looked in through the screen door of my room to ask how I was feeling—for of course Mr. Alderson had told them the story, sparing no details. They were properly sympathetic, yet I thought I noticed a gleam of amusement in their eye.

Now everyone knew that both Lew and the other man imbibed quite freely when they went to town. So I spoke up from the bed, as well as I could for my swollen and aching jaw, and I said: "I don't see how either one of you two men could ever go and get drunk more than once in your lives. Once is enough!"

Lew said: "Why, Nannie, the trouble is you got *too* drunk. You don't want to overdo it. You want to drink just enough so you feel you're on top of the world."

I said, "Thank you, I don't see where there is one single pleasant sensation connected with it!" And I didn't—except that one instant when the tooth came out.

Needless to say, I never heard the last of it.

If you have a particle of ambition in your system there is no rest on a ranch. Besides all the usual routine of cooking and washing and sewing, there are things to attend to that women in town don't try to do for themselves; such as making butter, and taking care of the meat. I stuck to my rule of not whining; indeed I was almost an Indian when it came to concealing my feelings. But I'm afraid my outlook on life was affected, nevertheless. I was not patient with the children. And I found I was taking dislikes to people. Mr. Alderson's boundless hospitality often rubbed me the wrong way.

I had never felt that way during the first years of our marriage, only on Muddy. It was the custom of our country to let people come and stay as long as they liked; but they were supposed to do a little work for their board; at least carry in some wood and water once in awhile. Half the time, however, our self-invited guests wouldn't do even that. I didn't in the least mind keeping them when they showed some appreciation of Mr. Alderson's open-handedness, but I felt very differently when they didn't appreciate it.

The time we were building the addition to the house, a man had been living with us, or on us, all winter. The men were hurrying to finish before the breeding season started on May 1, and there was just a little more daubing to do—that is, putting mud between the logs, and this man never offered to lift a finger. Finally Mr. Alderson said to him pointedly: "I will *pay* you the regular wages if you will finish the daubing on this side of the house." And he finally paid him a full day's wage for a half day's work.

The truth is that the country and the people in it were changing, or perhaps it was that the type of work on our ranch had changed. We no longer saw so much of cowboys, but had what seemed an endless procession of plain hired men, who were taken for the haying or some other temporary job. Half the time they were nice; the other half they were what Packsaddle Jack would have called pure scrubs. But they had to be treated like members of the family just the same.

I have often noticed that it is the little things that trouble a woman, while only the big ones trouble a man. Some of these men had table manners which got on my nerves. We had one guest for a season who always licked the spout of the syrup jug, after pouring the syrup on his hot cakes every morning.

I can't tell you how it affected me, to see this happen at my table every day. I begged Mr. Alderson to speak to the man, but of course he never would.

Again I think it was because a woman on a ranch was alone so much, that little things seemed big to her. Her hands were busy all day, but her mind was idle, with so few people to see, no radio to take her mind off herself, and very little to read. I would keep thinking of the same things over and over, until they nearly drove me crazy. Whenever Mr. Alderson was riding away from home, I was terribly afraid he would be killed by the Indians.

I know that I greatly magnified the danger, but real grounds for anxiety did exist.

Although the Crow Indian scare in the summer of '89 had come to nothing, for some time after that our own Indians, the Cheyennes, continued to give us trouble. The explanation was the usual one—"the young men are restless." Their attitude was ugly and menacing, and there was a great deal of stealing and butchering beef—though the government had given them a reservation on some of the best land in Montana, and regular issues of food.

In the summer of 1890 we had a nerve-racking thing happen. They killed a young cattleman named Bob Ferguson, because he had accidentally come upon them butchering a steer.

We knew Bob Ferguson slightly—a pleasant young

fellow, whom we'd seen at dances at the agency. He had been out hunting horses, and had been gone several days before his friends on the Rosebud missed him. As I said before, a man could easily be dead or injured for a long time, while his friends remained easy in the belief that he had stopped off at some ranch. When they made a search, they found his saddle horse shot to death in the bottom of a draw. They found no body at first, but they didn't waste time wondering what had happened.

My husband was not on the roundup that year, because he had cut his herd down to a small number of purebred cattle, which he watched closely near our ranch on Muddy. He was at home the day Frank Robinson came riding up to our house to tell us that Bob Ferguson had been murdered.

Mr. Robinson belonged to the firm of Carpenter and Robinson, the largest stockmen on the Rosebud, and was a fine and quiet though very forceful man. He told my husband that his outfit had stopped their roundup and moved over with all their cowboys to the scene of the crime, and he asked Mr. Alderson to go over and help with the search.

"Walt," he said, "none of our lives will be worth that if these Indians aren't brought to justice"— which was expressing just what I had always feared.

Mr. Alderson of course went with them. For a week they combed the country, riding over hillsides and up draws, searching every fold of the hills for signs that the earth had been disturbed. But the search concentrated near where the horse was found, for Mr. Ferguson was a tall man and they felt sure the Indians would not carry the body far. They were about to give up, when at last they found some finger marks in the dirt of the bank above a dry gully, and knew they were near their goal. They dug underneath, and found the body just where they expected it. The Indians, they figured out, had carried dirt in their blankets to cover it, had placed rocks on top of the dirt and had then scraped more earth down on top of that. Scouting out from there, they found empty cartridges behind some rocks, where the Indians had evidently waited for him and had shot him as he passed. When he started out to hunt his horses, Bob Ferguson had borrowed a pair of field glasses from a friend. From that, and from the fact that the remains of a butchered beef were found not far off, they concluded that he had been up on top of a hill somewhere, probably using the glasses to look for his horses; that the Indians down below him, cutting up the carcass of the stolen animal, had thought that he was spying upon them, and had murdered him out of fear.

No justice was ever done, in spite of the body being found. It was hard for white men to be positive, when testifying, in identifying any Indian; the Indians knew that, and took advantage of it. A buck named Whirlwind was arrested, because they found Bob Ferguson's knife in his shirt. But he was acquitted at the trial, largely through the efforts of a group of Indian sympathizers, led by none other than Father Vandervelden.

The murder of Bob Ferguson was so exactly in the image of my fears, that after it happened I was worse than ever. I was terrified lest Mr. Alderson might come upon some who were butchering cattle, as poor Mr. Ferguson had done, and become a marked man thereby. He was never delayed in getting home that I didn't suffer all the horrors that this fear wrought.

The year Bob Ferguson was killed or the year after, he went to the agency one day to transact some business. I expected him home at supper time, but he didn't come. The night grew later and darker, and still he didn't come. I kept trying to tell myself, "I know there's some reason." But I couldn't think of a single reason. For he knew how I worried, and I felt sure that if he had been detained he would have sent somebody.

The fact was that he had sent somebody, but the messenger chose to ignore his errand. As I learned later, Mr. Alderson found an Indian, among the crowd of bucks who congregated in front of the agency store, and paid him to ride over and tell me that Mr. Alderson would be detained. Hours afterwards my husband saw the Indian's horse still tied to a hitching rack, made inquiries, and found that he had never left town. It was then too late to do anything.

At home I had put the children to bed in their room, and Toby was in bed in the kitchen—though he said afterwards that he couldn't sleep because he knew how worried I was. I couldn't go to bed. I couldn't even sit down. I was more nervous than I have ever been before or since. I just kept walking up and down. All I could see was Indians lying in ambush to shoot him—for they knew he was one of those who had found the body of Bob Ferguson, and it was very likely that they would try to get revenge. I saw his body lying out there in the dark with a bullet through it. As I walked I would keep going to the window, though it was too dark to see anything, and I would listen and strain my ears to hear him coming—and the flies knocking against the ceiling sounded to me like distant horses coming, and I would think it was riders on their way to tell me he was killed.

We have a bird in this country that whistles at night, with a sound like a person whistling, and as Mr. Alderson whistled a good deal, when I heard that bird in the distance I would think it was he.

A stake horse, so-called, was always kept up at night—tied with a rope so he would be ready to go after the other horses in the morning. Toby and the other man had turned out the stake horse that night, because they thought Mr. Alderson would be home and would put his horse in the barn. But when Mr. Alderson didn't come, the two of them got up and went out with lanterns, and tried to find a horse on which to go hunt for him. That was just at the time he was nearly home, about 11 o'clock, and he said that as soon as he saw those two lights up on the hillside he knew what had happened.

When he came in, I looked so queer that he thought I was going to faint, and caught me in his arms. I said, "Nonsense, I've never fainted in my life."

That was the worst time I ever had, but there were many others. I was always nervous when he was late, and he was late a great deal. When a man was out riding after stock, there was no knowing when he would be home. He was not like a farmer, who comes in to regular meals; when the horses or cattle were not where he expected, he simply kept on riding until he found them.

The whole thing became a nightmare which never left me until we decided, in the fall of 1893, to give up our ranch and move to Miles City. How rejoiced I was at this decision! For in leaving the ranch I felt I was leaving this dreadful fear which had haunted me. I did put it behind me as soon as we reached Miles City, and spent the next year and a half without the shadow of apprehension on my mind. That was the dreadful irony.

Chapter XXI

IT WAS THE FALL OF 1893 WHEN WE LEFT OUR
ranch and moved to Miles City, and there were
several reasons for the move. For one thing, Mabel
was ten years old now and had never had any schooling except what the Montgomery Ward catalog had
given her. In our early day the school did not come
to the country to meet the child; instead the child
had to be taken into town to school. When it comes

to high school, parents have the same problem today, wherever ranches are far apart. But lonely little white school houses, rising out of the bleakest stretches of sagebrush, have solved it as far as the A, B, C's are concerned.

We made our move just after a wave of bank failures which swept the country. The panic of 1893 swallowed up, along with many others in Montana, the Stockgrowers National Bank in Miles City, and my husband's $6000 life-insurance policy was lost. It was the larger of two which he carried. On every side our friends had met reverses, as well as ourselves. Horses and cattle, we thought, had been low enough in price before, but they went much lower now. There was no demand for horses at all, then and for several years afterwards. Good ones brought five dollars or less in Miles City in 1895, and there was already much talk to the effect that this splendid animal was passing, and would soon be found only on exhibition in museums. It was very depressing.

The low prices were another reason why we gave up the ranch. It had become harder and harder to make ends meet there. So we turned it over to Toby Larsen and his brother to run. A third inducement which led us to go to Miles City was the promise of a well-paying position for Mr. Alderson. The sheriff was a friend of his, and had told him that if he came, he would give him work all year serving papers after ranch failures. But this never materialized.

In many ways our new life was a distinct step upwards—at least in the minds of the children! We had moved into a big, red frame house, in a big, ragged yard, on the outskirts of town. It had a furnace, a bathroom—and an upstairs! Not since Mabel was a baby had we lived in a two-story house; Patty, and of course Walter, who was too young to count, had never seen stairs, and Fay and Patty went up and down, up and down, all day.

We didn't furnish the upstairs because the lower part was big enough for us, and besides we didn't have enough furniture; not even when we had bought several additional pieces at a sale of officers' effects, when these officers and their families were leaving Fort Keogh. Among other things, we bought a magnificent folding bed for twenty-four dollars at the sale. It put my homemade efforts—which were merely hooked up under a shelf, and concealed by a curtain—forever to shame. For this bed, when not in use, looked like a buffet, with a mirror and shelves above, and drawers below. You could even keep bric-a-brac on the shelves—or could have, if you'd had any bric-a-brac. I never did have any. And when you pulled the handle of one of the "drawers," you released the bed. We kept this superb thing for twenty years, taking it with us on all our various moves, until finally, when it took to collapsing with our overnight guests, we cut it up into four separate pieces of furniture, ranging from a mirror to a porch swing.

Since we had no use for the upstairs rooms, the children could use them for playhouses. Thus each little girl rejoiced in the possession of a room of her own, where she could do exactly as she pleased. I believe if we had had a doorbell, their cup of happiness would have been full.

You see, they had heard of doorbells. And we did have one years later, when I had given up my attempts at being a business woman in Miles City and had gone back to live in Birney. At that time we had what our neighbors claimed was the first doorbell in eastern Montana, but I always thought that was a large order. A friend from Nebraska had brought it to us as a present, and we had installed it at our front door. It was a patented affair with a large, bronze knob, and rather complicated; the man who gave it to us was a salesman, and while I never knew, I always thought that the bell was part of his "line." As far as I can recall it was never rung but once. Nobody ever came to the front door on a ranch; people would leave their horses in the barn or at the hitching rack, and then use the back door.

But this one time some friends from Hanging

Woman came out to see us, and I saw them coming and stuck my head out the window and said: "Please go round to the front door and ring the bell." And they did.

Miles City was a place of delight to the children. But grownups can't look at things through fairy glasses, and to Mr. Alderson it was a scene of grave disappointments, at least for the first year. Times were very hard. Nothing brought in any money after the panic, though he was trying all the while to tide us over until the market went up for horses and mules. First he grubstaked two men to open up one of the small local coal mines for him, but they reneged on their agreement, and so no profit came to us from that. Just before we moved to Miles City he took up a homestead at the mouth of Tongue River canyon, planning to irrigate and raise oats there, and he also put in an irrigation ditch for Mr. Brown. He tried all the ways there were to bring in a little money. He used to say that he didn't understand how it was —that when he was a young man and money didn't mean much to him, everything he touched turned to it. But now that he was married and needed it so badly, it wouldn't come. But of course he failed to allow for the difference in the times.

Things were beginning to look better just before he was hurt. The first sign of upturn was such a little thing, it was hardly more than a joke, but it cheered us up, just the same. Mr. Alderson won the prize at a raffle. Surely this was a good omen, even though the prize was—another folding bed!

The furniture man in town had had in stock for some time this most elaborate bed, which he had doubtless bought before the panic. It was so expensive nobody would buy it, so he decided to raffle it off. On the night of the raffle there was a big crowd in the furniture store, and a young man rose to his feet and made a speech about Mr. Alderson, saying: "We all know Walt's been having a lot of hard luck lately. I'm going to shake the dice and win for him." Everybody cheered when he did.

This was the era of folding beds, as the reader by now will have guessed. But the one we acquired at the raffle topped them all. It folded up into something like a wardrobe, with a mirror clear down to the ground. For the first time since I left West Virginia, I was able to see my feet.

There were other signs, there toward the last, to make us feel that our luck was about to change. Friends were pulling hard for us, and the time came, as it is bound to do, when one of them was in a position to make his wishes effective. In 1894 our old partner, Mr. Zook, was elected county assessor, and he made Mr. Alderson his deputy. It was a fine position, and we felt now that everything would be all right.

And so it would have been, beyond a doubt in the world—if the dreadful and unlooked-for had not happened. There is no help in brooding over the evils dealt by fate, or in wondering why this or that was as it was. But it has always been a strange and bitter thought to me, that the anxieties about Mr. Alderson's safety, which haunted me so on the ranch, should have quieted when we came to Miles City. The presence of so many people around seemed to give me a feeling of security, and so, on the afternoon of the accident to my husband, I was happily busy, and had no premonition at all of the greatest tragedy that can come to a wife and mother.

But I must go back a week or more before it happened.

Coming home one afternoon, Mr. Alderson had said cheerily: "What do you think I bought today?"

My heart sank. I answered: "Not another beaded pincushion, I hope!"

The beaded pincushion was a family by-word. For, another time some years before, when we were just as hard up as we were now—and I needing curtains the worst way—Mr. Alderson had seen an old squaw offering this awful-looking thing for sale. She wanted five dollars for it, and looked so disappointed when nobody would buy, that he offered her a dollar— which she snatched at, you may be sure. So home he came with the beaded pincushion.

Now, as before, we were buying only what we absolutely needed and we had to do without a great deal of that. So no wonder I was dismayed when Mr. Alderson said: "What do you think I bought today?"

He went on to tell me that on his way home he had passed the sale corrals on Main Street, where Judge Brown, the livery stable keeper and a great friend of his, was holding an auction. To explain how a livery stable man came to hold the title of "Judge," I need only say that Judge Brown once had held office as justice of the peace. Mr. Alderson climbed up on the fence along with others to watch the sale, when Judge Brown turned to him and said: "Just look at this, Walt. Here is a four-year-old, not a blemish on him, gentle, and I'm only offered five dollars for him."

Mr. Alderson said: "Why, I'd give you seven."

It was the highest bid—and he came home leading the horse, which we named Seven Dollars.

The fact that we had any quantity of horses on the range, and good ones too, which we couldn't sell but on which we had to pay taxes, put this "buy" in the class with the beaded pincushion—no doubt about it.

But my husband, who was always optimistic, said: "I'll get my money out of Seven Dollars, for he's well broken, and I need a horse right now to drive with that filly, whose mate I had to shoot."

The loss of this filly had been one of many discouragements. She had slipped on the ice and broken her leg, but my husband had set her leg and put her in a swing, hoping to save her for breeding purposes. She was doing well when the swing slipped, and she was so badly hurt that she had to be put out of the way.

Since his appointment as deputy assessor Mr. Alderson knew that he should have many miles of traveling to do, not all of it on horseback, and for this reason he wanted to break in Seven Dollars as the other member of his team. On the day of the accident, he left early in the morning, driving the new horse and the surviving filly, and he asked me to come and open the gate leading out of the stable yard. I opened the gate, and the two horses started off as if they had always been driven together. When Mr. Alderson returned several hours later it was beginning to storm, and he called to me not to come out to open the gate, as the horses were gentle and would stand. The last time I saw him conscious, was when he got out of the light driving cart, holding the reins in his hand, opened the gate and went on into the stable.

With the unending optimism of ranchmen about horses, a friend of ours had just brought in a gaited stallion from Missouri, preparatory to breeding still more saddle animals for a five-dollar market. My husband had insisted upon his keeping the new horse in our stable, until he was rested sufficiently from his train trip to be taken out to the ranch. The stallion had been very restless and had been kicking and whinnying whenever anyone entered the barn. But I had thought nothing of it.

When Mr. Alderson didn't come to the house right away I thought that with his usual kindness to dumb animals, he was making them comfortable, even to currying them free of the slushy ice from the drive. So I went about my work while the two younger children were playing, and the older ones not yet home from school.

The first intimation I had of anything like a tragedy was when the living room door opened and our Doctor looked in, closing the door before I could speak to him. Opening the door again, I saw the Doctor and Sheriff Hawkins disappear around the house, saw them vault over the fence without waiting to open the gate. As I hurried to the back porch, another friend was coming to meet me, both hands reaching out in tender friendliness.

"Walt has been badly hurt," he said, "we think kicked in the head. You must be brave and help me."

I thought if he was kicked in the head the two babies must not see their father so, and I picked them up and ran across the street to a good neighbor, telling her the little I knew and asking that she keep them till I could come again for them. Then I helped Mr. Hastings get the bed ready. Then doctors and friends carried my husband in.

He had been found lying face downward on the stable floor, with the imprint of two horse's hoofs on his head. From the position of the horses when they found him, they argued that he must have let Seven Dollars go to his stall, while he was tying the filly; that Seven Dollars, being loose, had backed out and started kicking at the stallion, and as the fight broke out with that lightning-like fury, to which I had once been witness, Mr. Alderson was somehow caught between them.

They gave me no hope from the first, but as the days and nights passed and he became apparently more comfortable, I did hope in spite of all they said. All that our two good doctors and the surgeon from Fort Keogh could do was done, but the fracture extended to the base of the brain, and he was never himself again. He died after six days, on the 18th of March, 1895.

People were so kind, so incredibly kind; and one of the most faithful was our dear friend, Judge Brown, the auctioneer. He was at my husband's bedside from morning till night, it seemed, to the neglect of his business; there were still no nurses in Miles City, and strange as it may seem, the doctors turned to the big, uncouth-looking livery-stable keeper, rather than to some woman, when my husband had to be moved or an operation attempted.

Because it was winter and there was no active work on the range, the stockmen were all in Miles City, and they were in our house constantly. The second night after the accident, I saw a group of them talking in the dining room. Among them was a man whose family was keeping the older children, and who was also our life insurance agent.

He came to me and asked: "Do you know where Mr. Alderson's insurance papers are?"

I went to the desk and found the papers, and gave them to him. I saw him, back in the next room, unfold the papers while a crowd of men looked on, read through them, and heard one voice after another say: "Thank God."

He told me later that man after man had come to him with money, offering to fix up the insurance policy in case my husband had not kept it paid up— if it were not too late to fix it. When the seventh man came at midnight with money, he came to ask me for the papers!

Often and often since my husband's death, I have thought of how the sun came out the morning of our wedding day to shine so briefly and beautifully, only to disappear once more behind banks of purple storm clouds, as it settled in to rain that night. The rain lasted a long time—and that interval of sunshine has always seemed to me symbolic of our life together. It was so very short. The years since then have been close-packed and strenuous as before. But after my husband's death, I was no longer a bride who went west, nor a woman who was helping to open up a new country; I was merely on overworked mother of four, trying to make ends meet under conditions which were none too easy.

Chapter XXII

I DON'T LIKE TO LEAVE MY STORY ON A NOTE OF
sorrow, for there was so much afterwards that wasn't
sorrow. For seven years after Mr. Alderson's death
we lived in Miles City, where I did what I could to
support the children and myself. I ran a boarding
house; I made bread and sold it; I kept a cow and
sold the milk; I had a little catering business. I never
had any help except now and then a man to milk the

cow, and once in awhile an old darky woman—just about the only one in town—who lent a hand when I was getting up a supper for the Masons on Lodge nights. Mr. Alderson had been a Mason, and they were faithful customers. I always liked catering for men. They were always generous, and they never fussed about little things.

But I didn't have a speck of business ability, and I couldn't get ahead with any of it. My husband's life insurance policy paid me three thousand dollars, and I didn't do anything sensible with that, either—I just frittered it away, buying food for people, mostly. I had ten or twelve steady boarders, besides others who came in for dinners on Sunday, and somehow those boarders ate up a great deal of money. Between the work and the worry, I believe my friends thought I was going to lose what little sense I had. So they persuaded me to go back up Tongue River to Birney and open a store.

That was in 1902, and for the next few years I was mother, postmistress, and leading merchant of Birney. We lived in a log house of three big rooms which had formerly been the parsonage. It ought to have felt like home to us, for the logs which built it had come from my own old house on Tongue River. Birney looked like a town in a wild western movie—with its log houses, its wide, dusty street, and the horses tied to hitching racks in front of the stores. My customers were cowboys and Indians.

When the Indians came into the store, they would start out by changing all their money into nickels and dimes; they would then stuff it in their mouths, and spit it out, a coin at a time, as they made their purchases. I did a big volume of trade selling them lemon flavoring extract, which was priced at a dollar for one small bottle. One afternoon a big Indian bought a bottle of it. He came back staggering drunk an hour later, when he proceeded to unbuckle his six-shooter and swing it around under my nose, making me think that my last hour had come. It turned out, however, that he was merely trying to get at the silver dollars which he carried in his six-shooter belt, in order to buy more of the extract. I knew he didn't want it to put in cake. The government forbade the sale of fire water to the Indians—and the tiny vials of extract contained alcohol. But I'd had no idea until then that so small a quantity could produce such a startling effect.

My business ability was no better than ever. I had an awful time being postmistress because of the money orders, which were the bane of my life. And how I dreaded the visits of the postoffice inspector!

The duties of the merchant were complicated by those of the housewife and mother. With all the children to look after and cook for, I couldn't be in the store all the time, and when I wasn't in it, it had to be locked. I never had a cake in the oven, nor a caller with whom I particularly wanted to sit and visit, that a customer didn't come.

The first thing to be done was to let him in—and that involved finding the key. It was a great big iron thing about a foot long, but it managed to get lost just the same. So we tied a big piece of wood to it, and then we couldn't find the wood. It is *not* true, as my son Walter tells, that I never knew the price of anything in the store, nor that I told people to go in and help themselves and just write it down! The truth was bad enough. But I was grateful that the losses suffered from mismanagement were made up in part by friends like Shorty Caddell, a short, chunky Texan with a sharp tongue and a kind heart, who was foreman of the 3 X Bar. Shorty would bring me a quarter of beef whenever he came to town, and would threaten his boys with dire things if they didn't give their trade to "the pore widder woman."

If I lived in isolation for a few of my earlier years, I've been making up for it all the rest of my life. On mail days in Birney we saw everybody in the world— our own world, that is, which was small but humming. The country was becoming very civilized by that time; the mail came twice a week, and people would ride or drive in from their ranches and spend the day in town. So many would stop for a meal with us, that often we would have three and four settings at the table. Of course, the extra cooking made work. But hard work never hurt anybody, and neither did being tired. I have often thought that people who have never been tired don't know the blessed boon of rest.

In the summer, mail night was always dance night. Fay was going to high school in Miles City then, and she would bring her friends home to stay with her, and the five or six girls would draw all the unattached boys from up and down the river and over the divides. Often there would be fifty or sixty horses tied up to the hitching rack in front of the store. The dances were held in our living room, and there were always so many extra boys that some of them would have to tie handkerchiefs around their arms and take the girls' parts in the square dances.

We had a little piano which was played at all our parties, and at all the parties in the Tongue River country. It was a miniature Steinway, two octaves short, that had belonged to some friends of ours in Miles City. They had brought it out from New York for their little girl, and when they left and went east we bought it from them for twenty-five dollars. I believe it was made originally for some kind of exhibition, but I never really knew its earlier history.

I only know that when the family came west to live on a ranch, the piano was sent out by freight, on the Northern Pacific; that it was unloaded at Rosebud station, on the Yellowstone, a few miles west of Miles City, in the midst of those bleak, sagebrush-covered hills. It was fall then, and the river was running full, so for several weeks the little piano sat on the open station platform, protected only by its crate, while they waited for the river to freeze over so they could take it across. The experience didn't seem to hurt it any—though some of its sweetness of tone may have dwelt in the uncritical ears of those who listened to it.

At any rate, I am sure that no other Steinway ever made gave half the pleasure that little piano did. For years it was the only piano in the Birney country—until Captain Brown bought one for the Three Circle. Whenever my children went to a dance, the boys would load it in a wagon, throw a tarp over it in case of snow or rain, and off it would go. It was borrowed for parties by neighbors from miles around, and everyone loved it as though it were something alive. From time to time the cowboys talked of sending to Sheridan and getting somebody to come up and tune it. But for some reason this was never done, and the only time it was ever tuned was once when my daughter Mabel and a friend of hers took a monkey wrench and tightened up the strings.

After five years in Birney we made another move. By 1906 Mabel had married a man from the East and was living on a ranch on Young's Creek, farther up Tongue River. I borrowed money and bought one near her, and became a cattle queen, with thirty-five cows, and an outfit consisting of a thirteen-year-old boy and a girl.

Walter, my son, had started punching cows at the age of eleven. He first went on the roundup wearing black cotton stockings and bib overalls—the latter looked down upon as a style worn by farmers, not cowboys—because he was too little to be fitted with the proper clothes. But by the time he was thirteen he was a full-fledged cowpuncher drawing a man's wages. He ran the ranch winters, when he was at home, but during the spring, summer and fall, while he was gone, Patty and I ran it. We had help from kindly neighbors, but most of the man's work was done by Patty, who rode and roped, fixed fences and pitched hay. As her brother said, "she was the best hand on a horse I ever saw for a lady, though she was a little wild."

Loneliness was a thing of the past. For there were settlers all around us now—too many settlers, the cowmen said. They were a different type from the earlier ones. They were dry farmers, and many of them belonged to churches which didn't approve of dancing. But still the old life went on for a few more years, side by side with the new. We had two of the biggest cattle companies in southern Montana for neighbors, the Dana and Spear Brothers outfits, and our ranch became an unofficial headquarters for their cowboys, especially for the Spears. We had so many of them taking meals with us, that finally Doc Spear said to me:

"Mrs. Alderson, you keep track of the number you feed, and I'll pay you twenty cents a meal."

But I never worried about the margin of profit. Between the neighbors and the cowboys, we had visitors all the time. One night, I remember, Patty and I were alone, and were fixing a little supper for ourselves, and before we were through we had nineteen people.

We always kept open house for anyone who wanted to spend the night. A stranger coming into the house might wonder at first glance where we would put the extras—but ranch hospitality was organized along definite lines. First you filled the beds—three in a double bed being considered capacity. After that you simply peeled off the extra sougans and straw ticks and mattresses which you kept piled up on top of the beds, and spread them out on the floor. When it came to children, as the saying was, we'd simply hang them on a nail.

The end of ranching for me came in 1919. That was the terrible year of the drouth and the crash, which spelled disaster for so many in our country. Walter had built up our herd, by 1917, to 250 cattle, and after that, under the influence of the war boom, we had bought seven hundred head on money borrowed from the bank. When the market dropped we lost them all, and everything else with them.

And so we were broke again. It was hard for Walter to lose what he had worked so hard to build up, but he was young, and he still had his life ahead of him. While as for me, I was sixty years old, and I'd been broke so many times before that I could face it. When you have lived without money as much as I had, it loses a great deal of its power to hurt you.

Besides, all my children were married now except Fay, and she was teaching, and I had no one but myself to worry over. Instead of worrying, I went to live with Patty on Eaton's ranch. I have been there now for over twenty years, surrounded by friends and children, grandchildren, and lately a great-grandchild.

So the last twenty years have been serene ones. Before that, my friends tell me, I led a hard life. Perhaps—but I don't think an easy one is ever half so full.